Donaghadee Lifeboat

100 years of service

Contemporary logs
compiled and edited by
William Lennon BEM

BALLYHAY BOOKS

Published by Ballyhay Books,
an imprint of Laurel Cottage Ltd.
Donaghadee, N. Ireland 2009.
Copyrights Reserved.
© Text by William Lennon 2009.
All rights reserved.
No part of this book may be reproduced
or stored on any media without the express
written permission of the publishers.
Printed by Gutenberg Press Ltd., Malta.
ISBN 978 1 900935 79 1

Donaghadee Lifeboat

Contents

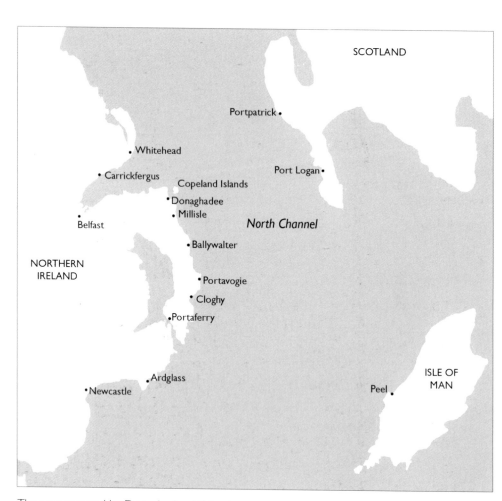

The area covered by Donaghadee Lifeboat

A Roll Call

William and Laura (1910-1931) Watson lifeboat, sails, 10 oars, petrol engine, 40 hp. Cost £3,599
carried out 61 launches and saved 65 lives.

Civil Service No. 5 (1932-1950) Watson lifeboat with a cabin for survivors, a stay sail, trysail, 4 oars and the new radio telephone. 2 x petrol engines, 60 hp, top speed 9 knots. She was built by John White of Cowes at a cost of £7,294.
Launched on service 80 times and rescued 56 lives

Sir Samuel Kelly (1950-1976) Watson design with a forward and after cabin. Diesel engines, 240 hp. Built by John White of Cowes at a cost £25,075.
Launched on service 134 times, 79 lives saved

Nelsons of Donaghadee 44-017 (1976-1977) Waveney Class, fast semi-planning hull used by the American Coastguard costing. 2 x 250 hp engines, top speed 15.5 knots. £200,000
Launched once, rescued 0

Arthur and Blanche Harris 44-006 (1979-1986) Waveney Class, semi-planning hull, 2 x 250 hp engines, top speed 15.5 knots. £200,000
Launched on service 81 times and rescued 41 lives.

City of Belfast 52-33 (1986-2003) Arun Class, second largest lifeboat in the RNLI all weather fleet. Cost £1.5 million. 2 x Caterpillar diesel engines, 485 hp, top speed 18 knots. Inflatable Y class boat on board for access to rocks or beach.
Launched on service 153 times, 35 lives saved

Saxon 14-36 (2003-present) Trent Class, 2 x MAN diesel engines, 860 hp, top speed 25 knots. Inflatable XP boat on board powered by a 5 hp outboard engine can be deployed to gain access to rocks or beaches where necessary.

The Coxswains

1910	Robert McDowell
1910	William George Nelson
1917	Andrew White
1940	Samuel Nelson
1941	James Davidson
1950	Hugh Nelson
1954	Alexander Nelson
1959	John Trimble
1967	George Lindsay
1967	Jim Bunting
1983	William Lennon
1991	Graham McConnell
1995	David Martin
1999	Philip McNamara

Donaghadee Lifeboat
Crew of 2009

Coxswain	Philip McNamara
2nd Coxswain	John Ashwood
Mechanic	Shane McNamara
Assistant Mechanics	John Allen
	George Hackworth
Crew	George Thompson
	Michael Fields
	Richard McGimpsey
	Stephen McComisky
	Alfie McCulla
	Mark Nelson
	Ross Bennett
	David McCormick
	Tony Simmons
	John Petrie

Author's note:

I would like to acknowledge the following people: Hugh Nelson, Gordon Nelson, Alan Roberts, Arthur Arbuckle, Kathleen Simpson, Walker Simpson MBE, Brett Cunningham, Sadie Allen, Alan Couser, Shane McNamara, Stephen Cameron, Ken Walsh, Rick Tomlinson, Ethel Petersen, Bill Pollock. To anyone I may have forgotten: thank you.

Donaghadee Lifeboat
An Introduction

In 1823 Sir William Hillary, an aristocrat and lifeboat man from the Isle of Man, wrote his Appeal to the Nation which led to the foundation of the modern lifeboat service. Although there were lifeboats around the coast, they were few and far between and independently run. The Appeal pointed out the loss to the nation from shipwreck and misery caused by so many deaths and the effect on the morale of all seamen. His Appeal gained widespread sympathy and support and in a meeting on 4th March 1824 at the City of London Tavern, the 'National Institution for the Preservation of Life from Shipwreck' was formed. In 1854 the name was changed to the Royal National Lifeboat Institution.

Donaghadee is a small town in County Down situated on the east coast of Northern Ireland about eighteen miles from Belfast and six miles from Bangor. It has a population of approximately 6,500 people. The lifeboat station at Donaghadee, founded in 1910, is one of the most important on the Irish coast. It was originally thought to be an ideal location due to the amount of shipping which used the Irish Sea to and from ports such as Belfast, Bangor and Donaghadee. There was also a thriving fishing community along the coast which has suffered many tragedies over the years at sea.

Historically the lifeboat was manned from the fishing community who were all experienced seamen. However, as the fishing industry in Donaghadee declined over the years, the lifeboat crew has been manned by many volunteers from many different professions. These volunteers give freely of their time and effort to be available for exercises and emergency calls to provide an excellent service to those in need at sea.

As the reader will notice, calls in the early years carried out by Donaghadee Lifeboat were mostly in very bad weather to give assistance to large sailing vessels. Then came the steamship era, and these calls were usually to large vessels, especially during wartime. In recent years the types of calls have changed again to mostly small leisure craft. Nowadays there is an ever-growing population who use the sea for many types of leisure activities such as sailing, water skiing, jet skiing and fishing. The RNLI has been successful in being able to adapt to these shifts by changing the types of lifeboats they design and in the crew training. Beach lifeguards have been a very successful recent addition to the work of the RNLI, which operates over 140 lifeguard units around the coast of the UK and have saved more than 60 lives and assisted nearly 10,000 people.

Training lifeboat crews has changed dramatically over the years; much of the training is now carried out in the Lifeboat College in Poole in Dorset and provides the skills required to man the lifeboats. Approximately 2,000 crew pass through the college annually to participate in one or more of the 36 different courses currently on offer.

All-weather lifeboat courses include search and rescue, boat-handling and preparation courses for the RYA Yachtmaster and Coastal Skipper exams. These courses are conducted afloat in bespoke Hardy training boats or in the purpose-built mission simulator. Complete darkness, thunder, lightning, and helicopter recovery can all be simulated to very real effect. The pool also hosts the capsize training element of inshore lifeboat courses.

Looking back over the years I wonder what the first lifeboat men in Donaghadee would have thought of the current lifeboats and the training provided.

Some interesting facts about the RNLI...

• The Royal National Lifeboat Institution is a registered charity that saves lives at sea. It is maintained entirely by voluntary contributions, fund-raising events and legacies for its income.

• It provides, on call, a 24 hour lifeboat search and rescue to 100 nautical miles out from the coast of the United Kingdom and Republic of Ireland, and a seasonal lifeguard services in many parts of the country.

• There are over 230 lifeboat stations strategically placed around the UK and the Republic of Ireland. Since the RNLI was founded in 1824, its lifeboat crews and since 2001, its lifeguards, have saved over 137,000 lives.

• The demand on lifeboat services is increasing yearly, for example lifeboat rescues have doubled since 1980. The trends in lifeboat work have changed dramatically over the past 100 years, which is due to much improved navigational aids and safety features in shipping today, however the increase in leisure activities such as sailing, power boating and jet skiing continues to keep the lifeboat busy especially during the summer months.

...and specifically Donaghadee lifeboat

• Donaghadee has made a worthy contribution to saving lives at sea during the past 100 years. One such notable service involving the RNLB *Sir Samuel Kelly* was on 31st January 1953 when the lifeboat rescued thirty three survivors from the Irish Sea from the stricken Larne-Stranraer car ferry, *MV Princess Victoria.*

• The *Sir Samuel Kelly,* while on relief duty at Courtmacsherry, was involved in another famous service during the 1979 Fastnet race when fifteen competitors were lost during a severe storm.

• The *Sir Samuel Kelly* can now be found in the car park at Donaghadee Marina where it awaits a permanent home in a purpose-built Lifeboat Museum in the town.

• Donaghadee had the first female crew member in the UK on an off shore lifeboat. Ruth McNamara (née Lennon) served from October 1984 to October 2004, during which time the lifeboat rescued 84 lives. There are now over 200 lifeboat woman in the UK and Ireland.

• Donaghadee Lifeboat has had a long and distinguished history and is well supported by the people of the town. The lifeboat crew, fund-raisers and supporters of the RNLI work tirelessly to raise much needed funds to support the work of the RNLI. They will undoubtedly go from strength to strength.

• *Lifeboat Luke,* Northern Ireland's first home-produced animated children's television series features a lifeboat in a fictional town called Donaghadoo. This series is a unique partnership with the RNLI; it is fast, fun and full of eccentric characters loved by all. It is not all fun and games as serious sea and beach safety messages underline each episode. Who knows, today's *Lifeboat Luke* fans could be our future lifeboat crew members!

Good luck to all involved in the sterling work of the RNLI in the future.

The Beginning

The *Ulrica* which met her end on the North Rock at the Copelands
Photograph courtesy of the Ian Wilson Collection

In 1897 sailing ship *Ulrica* was grounded at the Copelands on the North Rock at Old Lighthouse island. She was loaded with 3000 tons of grain from Sydney, Australia bound for Dublin and had been under tow by a Glasgow tug when her tow parted and her voyage ended on North Rock.

In 1901, the barque *Meridian* struck the Foreland Spit, Groomsport. A lifeboat

Tommy Simpson

was brought along the road to the Warren but could not launch because of the weather. Eight local fishermen brought a rowing and sailing yawl *Lucy* to the bay just north of the Foreland Perch called the Clear Hole and were able to make the very rough passage to the *Meridian*. Once the men boarded the ship they were able to help the exhausted crew. Later that day a tug arrived and towed the *Meridian* to Belfast. The men who made this hazardous journey were William George Nelson, Robert McDowell, William John Nelson, William McDowell, John Nelson, John McDowell, Robert Bunting and John Dunwoody.

On December 31st 1905, the ketch *Catherine Rainey* came ashore in Coalpit Bay adjacent to where the tennis courts and bowling greens are now in Donaghadee. The Ballywalter lifeboat was alerted and was transported by road with horses but could not launch because of the gale. Coastguards tried firing rocket lines but these were swept away in the strong wind. As time passed the ship started to break up and sadly all four crewmen were lost. The bodies were recovered and buried in unconsecrated ground at Movilla cemetery in Newtownards. A local collection was organised and the men now rest in the Parish Churchyard in Donaghadee.

On November 15th 1906, a tragedy occurred when three local fishermen drowned when their boat foundered off Ballyferris Point near Ballywalter. They were John McDowell and his son Robert McDowell. The third man was named Thomas Morrison. John McDowell is believed to be one of the men who went out in the *Lucy* to the *Meridian*.

After these and lesser incidents thoughts turned to trying to have a lifeboat stationed at Donaghadee with its fine harbour. Meetings were arranged in the town and eventually a committee was formed; two of the members were the local squire, Colonel Daniel De Lacherois, and the Rev R. H. Coote who was himself a keen sailor. After several years corresponding with the RNLI it was agreed to send a few Donaghadee fishermen on a fact-finding mission. Three men were chosen: William George Nelson, Robert Bunting and Captain Robert McDowell. They visited Dungarven, Fenit, Dun Laoghaire, Arklow and Wicklow. When the men returned they were quite sure that a motor lifeboat was needed to combat the strong tidal streams around Donaghadee. This was in 1909. The committee contacted RNLI and awaited their decision. In early 1910 it was announced Donaghadee would get one of the most up to date lifeboats early in the summer. The new boat was a 43 foot Watson fitted with a 40 hp petrol engine which also had sails and ten oars. The boat cost £3,599 and was paid from the legacy of Miss A. W. Clarke-Hall.

A crew was selected to go and bring the new boat home. They were William George Nelson, Thomas Simpson, Jamie McDougal, David Majury, Billy Davidson and James Taylor, a local car engineer. A trip to London and staying in hotels was a new and exciting time for these young men. Their journey from London to Harwich was broken with an overnight stay in Yarmouth on Sands.

When they arrived, Tommy Simpson spied a counter offering whelks in vinegar in the foyer and he thought the lads would like a go at these. When they arrived at their table they discovered these whelks were what they knew as buckies, an animal they used everyday to bait their long lines. So now the problem was how to dispose of them. Somebody remembered seeing a guy playing a trumpet outside the hotel; he was duly tempted with these goodies and was delighted to take them off their hands.

The porter, on showing the men to their rooms, told them that if they required their shoes to be cleaned they just had to leave them outside their room door. Now Tommy Simpson was a small man with very small feet and when the shoe polisher noticed the pair of ladies' shoes outside he informed the manager that there must be a woman who had not registered in the room. Tommy had to be approached but when the manager saw Tom's small feet he was satisfied as to the owner of the shoes.

On arriving in Harwich the men were met by RNLI personnel Lieutenant Commander McClean and a Mr Small, an engineer, who were to sail with them. The men were under instruction not to sail at night or in fog. Their first stop on their passage north was Grimsby, Scarborough, then on to Tynemouth, Berwick-on-Tweed, Grangemouth, then through the Bowland Canal and into the Clyde, stopping in Troon. Leaving the next day for their home station after a passage lasting 11 days they arrived on 10th July 1910 to a splendid welcome from the townspeople.

Captain Robert McDowell was appointed coxswain with an annual payment of £12. William George Nelson was appointed 2nd coxswain with a payment of £6. A stipulation to being coxswain that was that he had be at the ready at all times and must not act as pilot for ships or take charge of a yacht. Captain McDowell felt he could not comply with this rule and severed his connection with the RNLI, being replaced by the 2nd coxswain. This rule was rescinded a few years later.

Sadly William George was drowned along with another young man named Majury in November 1917 when the boat they were in capsized while they were out fishing for lobsters. Andrew White was promoted to coxswain and went on be one of the longest serving coxswains in the RNLI from 1917 until 1949.

Donaghadee Lifeboat
William and Laura

The *William and Laura.* Crew members: J. White, H. Nelson, D. Nelson, J. Bunting Snr, T. Simpson, S. Nelson, A. McWilliams, A. Nelson

September. The naming ceremony of Donaghadee's first lifeboat was held in September 1910. Mr Charles Dunbar Buller, president of the Donaghadee branch and Miss Slade, representing the late donor, handed the boat over.

A short time after taking up station *William and Laura* got her first call to *Agamemnon* of Plymouth just south of Portavogie at the North Rock. She stood by the vessel until the tug *Ranger* took her in tow.

1910

William George Nelson,
Coxswain 1910-1917

1911

November 6. Assisted schooner *Mary* of Glasgow.

November 23. Gave help to *SS May* of Belfast.

1914

February 11. Stood by schooner *Kate* of Castletown.

Just four days later an alarm was raised that a ship was ashore on Shaws Rock north of Ballyferris Point. The lifeboat launched with William George Nelson in charge and proceeded at full speed to the casualty. On arrival they discovered the barque *Inverurie* of Aberdeen hard on the rocks and making water rapidly. The problems that faced the coxswain were the weather and the large crew of the ship, and so he decided to make two trips. A successful rescue was completed and twenty two crewmen were saved.

1915

March 18. This next call out sadly did not have such a happy ending. The small coaster *Upas* of Newry capsized in a gale off Burial Island. Luckily another ship, a collier called *Ailsa Craig,* was passing and noticed their plight. They launched a small boat with three men aboard into the rough sea and with great tenacity and skill managed to pull aboard two men but by this time all five men were exhausted. Just in time the lifeboat arrived and took the men aboard. Sadly the rest of the crew of the *Upas* foundered with their vessel.

November 9. The next call for the lifeboat was when *HM Transport No 90* went ashore on Skullmartin Reef. They were only required to stand by until the vessel refloated on the incoming tide without having sustained any serious damage and was able to continue her journey.

November 12. Just three days later *William and Laura* was called out to what was to be the most notable and dangerous exploit so far. The ship was the French ketch *Cyrano* of Brest and it was observed struggling southward in a ferocious gale. Watch was kept on the vessel and when she was abeam of Millisle the main mast and sails were carried away. *William and Laura* was alerted and after some difficulty cleared the harbour and headed out into the teeth of the gale. With William George Nelson at the helm, they battled towards the casualty. On reaching it they discovered the main mast was still attached to the ship and was punching holes in the hull. With a great amount of skill in such awful conditions the coxswain brought the lifeboat alongside. The crew of six were all saved and each member of lifeboat crew was awarded a certificate and a medal from the French Government in recognition of their skill and gallantry.

1916

September 27. Stood by *SS Cliffmore.*

1917

November 2. Schooner *Ellen Fisher* of Fleetwood put up distress signals and once again the lifeboat launched and rescued four crew.

November 28. Word reached Donaghadee Harbour-Master that a ship had been torpedoed about six miles off Donaghadee. He quickly alerted the crew and, with Andrew White in charge, launched the lifeboat. On reaching the scene they saw that the vessel, the *SS Aginoria,* was settling low in the water. Also alongside was a Naval patrol trawler which had taken aboard 10 men from the ship's lifeboat. The lifeboat got a further six aboard her leaving the captain and chief engineer on the ship. With the trawler standing by the coxswain decided to land the sixteen crewmen in Donaghadee. After refuelling, the lifeboat returned to the casualty to find that another trawler had turned up and the two trawlers had the vessel under tow. The captain said he required no further assistance and the *William and Laura* returned to station.

Andrew White,
Coxswain 1917-1950

1918

March 16. Stood by ketch *Pride of Mourne*.

September 21. *HMS Lifting Barge LC1.* A message was received from the Coastguard that a barge was ashore near Portavogie with six men aboard. The weather at the time was a full gale from the south-west with a very heavy sea running as it was low water and the flood tide was against the wind. When the lifeboat approached they saw the casualty was not ashore but had her anchors down which were dragging. Coxswain White then felt that for the men's safety he would have to bring them aboard as soon as possible. When this was done they steamed for Donaghadee and left the barge to her own devices. As far as is known she was boarded the next day and continued on her way.

1919

No call outs.

1920

December 3. *SS Thrushfield* of Londonderry. Coastguards alerted the Branch Secretary that a steamer was drifting ashore near their lookout at Orlock. The Secretary mustered the crew but when they got to the lifeboat ladder they saw the boarding boat had been sunk by the north-east gale which was causing large seas to break over the harbour wall. Luckily one of the crew had his fishing yawl tied nearby so it was brought into service to get aboard the lifeboat. It was a hard struggle through the Sound but eventually the casualty was reached. As her anchor was still dragging, the captain asked the lifeboat to come alongside and take off some of his men. Only three came aboard, the rest opting to stay on the ship. As the vessel was still in very serious danger, the lifeboat stood by.

Eventually the engineer managed to get the engine working again, proceeding to Donaghadee harbour with the lifeboat following. On this service the lifeboat was slightly damaged.

March 10. Stood by *SS Brynmoor.*

1921

December 30. A message was received from John Watterson, a fisherman from Groomsport, that a barquentine was flying distress signals about three miles north east of Groomsport.

William and Laura was launched and after clearing Donaghadee Sound the lifeboatmen got their first sight of the casualty. She had her anchors down and most of her sails were blown away. The weather on this occasion was heavy snow showers with a gale force north-westerly wind and, when the lifeboat got close, the captain shouted that he wanted himself and his crew taken off as he feared they would drag ashore on the Copelands. The seven men were taken off *Galic* and brought to Donaghadee. Next morning with the gale moderated, *Galic* was found to have dragged into Donaghadee Sound, having missed grounding on the Copeland Island, where she was boarded and towed to the harbour.

At 10pm the same night a ketch *New Leader* of Ramsey dragged her moorings in the harbour and was making distress signals. It was such a wild night no other boat could be used so the lifeboat crew was called and the lifeboat with nine crew aboard quickly got alongside the casualty and rescued three men and, while this was completed very sharply, it took two hours to put the lifeboat back on her mooring such were the conditions.

March 25. Stood by *SS Raylight* ashore on Ballyferris Point until it refloated.

1922

November 9. *SS Castle Island.* The Coastguard on watch at Orlock con-

1923

The *William and Laura*. Crew members: (l-r): Tommy Simpson, Willie White, Alex Nelson, Alfie McWilliams, Sammy Nelson, Hugh Nelson, Bobby Simpson. Front: Davy Nelson. Missing: Coxswain Andrew White

tacted the Honorary Secretary to say that a ship was in distress at South Briggs Reef. When the lifeboat arrived coxswain Andrew White realised this was going to be a difficult rescue – the ship was submerged with only part of the forecastle and the bridge showing, and it was here that the men were sheltering as the seas were breaking over it. He tried to get alongside the wheelhouse but was unable to because of the surge of the swells. He then attempted to put the bow of the lifeboat in and get the men to jump aboard; the first man mistimed his jump and was washed overboard Quick action by the lifeboat crew pulled him aboard again. While this was going on the lifeboat was taking a pounding against the ship and sustained considerable damage to her bow. Also just after leaving the casualty the lifeboat's engine began to overheat because of an airlock and had to be stopped. The rest of the trip was completed under sail. This was my father-in-law John Trimble's first service in the lifeboat and he told me of this difficult rescue of nine seamen.

1924   No launches.

1925   May 27. A fisherman's wife contacted the Honorary Secretary saying she was worried about her husband who had gone fishing the previous night

The Nelson brothers. Back row (l-r): John, Willie and Samuel. Front (l-r): William George and Frank

and had not returned.

The west south-westerly wind was very squally with heavy rain showers, and the coxswain agreed to launch. He proceeded to the usual fishing grounds, but finding nothing decided to search round the islands. Eventually the man was found sheltering on Mew Island safe and well. He and his boat safely returned to Donaghadee.

There were two other launches this year which only required the lifeboat to stand by.

No rescues.

1926

No rescues.

1927

March 21. Stood by *SS Deal* of London.

1928

1929 **September 28.** Stood by *SS Albia* of Bilbao.

1930 No rescues.

1931 **April 30.** Fishing yawl *Mercedes,* the coxswain's own boat being skippered by his son, on passage from Portpatrick, lost its propeller in mid channel. The lifeboat towed it to Donaghadee. This was the last rescue by *William and Laura.* She carried out 61 launches and saved 65 lives.

Donaghadee Lifeboat
Civil Service No. 5

Civil Service No. 5

The time had come to replace *William and Laura* and the Institution decided to upgrade the Station with another new Watson lifeboat 45'6" x 12'0" x 6'4" with a cabin for survivors, twin petrol engines, a stay sail, trysail, four oars and the new radio telephone. She was built by John White of Cowes at a cost of £7,294. This money was provided by the Civil Service Fund and the boat was to be named *Civil Service No. 5*.

Nothing is known about her delivery trip home. Her first year at home seems to have been very quiet too.

1932

1933

January 31. This is the same date that 20 years later that Larne would suffer a terrible disaster. An urgent request for lifeboat assistance came from Larne Harbour saying that one of Hood's motor boats had got blown out to sea with one man aboard. *Civil Service* left Donaghadee at 9.35 am. The weather at this time was gale force from west south-west with rain showers, and it took the lifeboat two hours to reach the area.

They searched a very wide area well into the night, and the coxswain decided at 3.30 am to give the crew a rest and a chance to get some food. He proceeded to Larne Harbour, leaving again at 6.30 am. The search was later called off by the Coastguard and the lifeboat returned to station at 10.30 am on 1st February. The coxswain said the boat behaved excellently and the crew were well pleased with her. Sadly the boat's occupant was lost.

1934

September 15. Saved small row boat and three persons.

1935

January 26. *SS Emma Sauber* of Hamburg lost her anchors and drifted ashore at Carnalea. Lifeboat guided vessel to safety and stood by.

May 15. Gave assistance to Bangor yacht *Morna*.

August 16-18. *SS Letitia* of Glasgow went ashore in dense fog. The Coastguard on Orlock Head knew from the very deep sound of the vessel's horn that she was close but could not see her. *Civil Service* was instructed to make for the Briggs Reef as this was the most likely place for her to be ashore. The lifeboat carefully felt its way past Orlock when suddenly out of the fog loomed this massive liner hard aground in a sandy bay called Betts Bay. On going alongside, 2nd coxswain Hugh Nelson who was in charge saw the ship's name and realised that she was one of the Anchor Donaldson line of trans-Atlantic liners carrying 300 passengers and 200 crew. If they had to go ashore they couldn't have chosen better, this place having a nice sandy bottom. As the tide was rising the captain tried to back the ship off using her own power but to no avail; she was stuck fast. The lifeboat stood by until the passengers had been transferred to another ship and, as the ship was in no danger, left the scene returning to station at 3 pm on the 17th. They were called to the liner again at midnight for another attempt at refloating with tugs. It was also unsuccessful and they returned home at 4 am. Next day the crew were paid off and the liner was handed into the care of four tugs to await a suitable tide for refloating. *Letitia* was towed off with hardly any

Front row (l-r): Commander Dutton, James Davidson, Andrew White, Hugh Nelson, Alec Nelson. Middle (l-r): Hugh Ferguson (white shirt), David McKibbon, Alec Hamilton, Bobby Simpson. Back (l-r): Jim Armstrong, Tommy Simpson.

damage done after four days aground.

June 22. *Star of Ulster* engine breakdown, towed in.

October 24. *Courageous* engine breakdown, towed in.

1936

November 19. A south south-easterly gale was blowing when *Civil Service* was launched after a message was received from Cloughey lifeboat station saying that a three masted schooner was in distress having lost two of her masts and all her sails approximately three miles east of Guns Isle. They were having great difficulties in launching the Cloughey lifeboat owing to the onshore gale.

The Donaghadee boat battled her way southwards covering the twenty some miles in three hours, arriving at the casualty to find the Cloughey lifeboat, a small Liverpool class, standing by having found it impossible to tow the ship, which was loaded with 135 tons of timber.

Coxswain Andrew White manoeuvred the lifeboat close to the stricken vessel and told the captain his intention was to tow his vessel with the

1937

two lifeboats and, as there was two hours floodtide left, they would make for Strangford Lough. Tow ropes were made ready and the tow began. Nothing in the records show if there were any dramas on the way in, only to say they arrived successfully in Portaferry Harbour at 12 midday. After the ship was safely moored, *Civil Service* left for home, arriving back at about 4.30 pm.

December 11. The Coastguard in Donaghadee went to the lifeboat house and fired the maroons and assembled the crew, informing Coxswain White that the lookout on Orlock Head had observed a vessel burning distress flares in the vicinity of Ballymacormick Point. The lifeboat left her moorings at 7.25 pm. The wind force was northerly 8 to 9 and the tide was ebbing causing very steep seas at the top of Donaghadee Sound and round the South Briggs Buoy. The lifeboat carried on into Groomsport Bay and slowed down to search the area at 7.55 pm. The flying spray and pitching boat made it very difficult to see anything but on getting closer to the point a lot of lights were seen along the shore.

Still they could not find any trace of a casualty. After searching the area for over two hours they noticed the lights on the shore gradually disappearing. They returned to station where they were met by Mr McKibbin, Honorary Secretary, who had been along at Ballymacormick Point and told them a ship called *Annagher* owned by John Kelly and Sons of Belfast had capsized and foundered. He said some bodies had been recovered on shore; out of a crew of 10, only one survived.

1938

October 9. Just one call this year, ironically to the coxswain's own boat *Mercedes* which had suffered an engine failure. Towed to Donaghadee, saved boat and five persons.

1939

January 9. Stood by local boat *Laura*. While the lifeboat was on this service another boat was seen to be having difficulties with the squally conditions – the *Prospector* from Ballywalter was escorted to Donaghadee harbour.

December 21. An armed trawler *Sir John Lister* was reported to be ashore on South Briggs Reef. When the lifeboat came alongside the coxswain asked what assistance they required. The captain asked if the lifeboat could shoot an anchor about 200 fathoms astern of his ship which was soon carried out. The weather at the time was very calm but foggy and the tide was at half ebb. As the vessel was in no immediate danger the

Samuel Nelson,
Coxswain 1940-1941

lifeboat was released. The trawler was refloated at high water with the aid of tugs.

As this was war-time many of the local fishermen and lifeboat crew were employed in Belfast Lough as pilots and boatmen. Almost all the local fishing boats were taken over by the Admiralty and moved to Belfast and Bangor to attend the ships assembling for convoys. On 1st July 1940 Samuel Nelson was promoted coxswain, 2nd coxswain James Davidson, Bowman Robert Simpson. Maroons were not being fired at this time and crews had to be contacted by motor car.

1940

July 20. *SS Troutpool* struck a mine in Belfast Lough with thiry seven crew aboard and all haste was made to reach the scene. They saw on arrival that the ship was in a sinking condition; they circled round the vessel a few times but could not see anyone aboard. Eventually they got a message that the ship's crew had got ashore in Bangor in their own lifeboats.

August 14. A message was received from Mr W. J. Burch of Millisle that he had seen a small yacht *Penguin* with two small boys aboard being blown out to sea by a fresh south-westerly wind. They were offshore at Ballywhiskin, so the crew were called and *Civil Service* got underway

Civil Service No. 5

heading for a point about three miles off the coast.

Nearing the position they could see a small rowing boat with two men in it trying to tow the yacht against the stiff breeze. The men and boys gladly accepted a trip back to shore at Millisle.

November 6. At 10.45 pm Polish steamer *Levant* ashore on Wilson's Point, Bangor with thirty crew aboard. The captain asked the coxswain if he would stand by until the tugs came as his ship was holed. Stood by until 9 am.

November 21. At 6.30 am a message was received from Donaghadee Coastguard that a ship was ashore on Ballymacormick Point. The weather was atrocious, the wind was hurricane force west north-westerly and to make matters worse the tide was ebbing; the lifeboat had trouble getting away from the mooring. Soon they were through the Sound and on nearing the Point they saw the *SS Coastville* hard on the rocks; it was obvious from the angle the ship was lying it would be impossible to get alongside in the lee of the ship. So the decision had to be made to attempt an approach on the weather side. With heavy seas breaking over the vessel and a great piece of boat handling, coxswain Samuel Nelson managed to lie alongside long enough to get seven of the nine crewmen aboard the lifeboat, the remaining two men went ashore by Breeches Buoy. Just as the lifeboat was struggling to pull away from the wreck, a tremendous wave hurled her against the ship's side breaking the mast which fell on the master, Captain Hughes, causing a severe head injury. It was decided then to take the survivors to Bangor to get Captain Hughes to hospital.

December 6. A message from the Coastguard stated that another ship, *Hope Star,* was aground on nearly the same part of Ballymacormick Point as before, so a new crew was mustered – they were certainly being kept busy with bad weather services. The wind that morning was not as vicious as the previous call but it was still blowing from the north-west force 8 to 9. It was almost a repeat of the last rescue; the coxswain had to battle with very heavy swells alongside trying to hold position to get the men onto the lifeboat. *Hope Star* had a crew of forty three but only nine decided to leave the ship, the rest elected to stay aboard. The lifeboat landed the crewmen in Bangor and, as the ship was holed, returned to stand by the rest of the day until the wind moderated, returning to station at 4.30 pm.

For these two services coxswain Samuel Nelson was awarded the RNLI Bronze Medal.

January 29-30. *SS Alhena* of Rotterdam. The Cloughey Honorary Secretary requested the assistance of Donaghadee lifeboat on this service as this ship had sixty persons aboard. The ship was loaded with 5,000 tons of supplies for 8th Army in Egypt bound from Liverpool to Port Said.

1941

Civil Service left the moorings at 8 am and was on scene just before 10 am. The Cloughey boat had started to land some of the passengers and crew.

The evacuation of the ship continued, the lifeboat boat landing fifteen survivors at Donaghadee and standing down at 5.30 pm. At 11 pm that night the Coastguards requested the lifeboat stand by at the wreck at first light to transfer secret papers and mails to an HM trawler. Among the many bags of mail were several large cases addressed to the King of Egypt. The work continued until the worsening weather made it too dangerous to stay. The *Alhena* was abandoned to her fate which was total destruction. Her bow can still be seen to this day showing above water just south of Portavogie.

April 15. At midnight a strange request was received from the Coast-

James Davidson,
Coxswain during the war

guard to launch the lifeboat and wait alongside to take aboard an armed guard. Soon the guard arrived consisting of 11 men and one officer who told the coxswain to put to sea – all very hush hush. Shortly after leaving harbour they were told to go to Mew Island where the soldiers disembarked. After a couple of hours they returned still not saying what they had been searching for, or if they had found it. The lifeboat arrived back in harbour about 3.30 am. This service was carried out by coxswain James Davidson, his first service after being promoted as coxswain during the War.

1942

January 20. A message was received that a coalboat *MV Kerin* had sunk one mile from Orlock Head and men were seen clinging to a life-raft. When the lifeboat reached the scene visibility was poor with fog banks. After a wide search the raft was found but unfortunately it was empty. There had been a crew of nine on board but no record of how they got ashore. Sadly the men on the raft were presumed drowned.

February 10. Escorted motor boat *Laura*.

1943

January 11. 1.15 am. A four-masted schooner *Ruth 2nd* loaded with 400

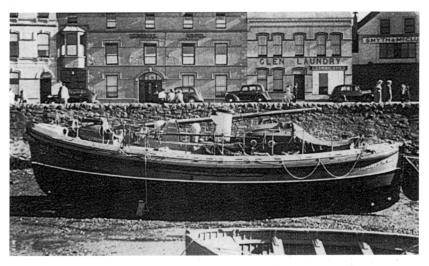

Civil Service No. 5 with Donaghadee in the background

tons of coal was driven ashore at Ballyvester about a mile from Donaghadee Harbour. The wind was gale force with very heavy seas. It took the lifeboat only fifteen minutes to reach the wreck but by that time she had been forced over the outlying rocks by the huge waves.

It was now impossible for the lifeboat to get near her. Meanwhile onshore, people were gathering to try and help. The ship now had washed in closer to the beach and Captain Larsen, after several attempts, managed to throw a rope ashore, making his end fast to a small raft which they launched and the shore helpers pulled ashore with two men clinging on. This was repeated a few more times but during one of these trips one man was washed off and was drowned. Captain Larsen was the last man to leave the ship and the lifeboat returned to harbour at 4 am. I remember this tragic event well as my father and I went along to see the wreck the next morning. Later a local man, Mr John Bennett, bought the wreck and broke her up to salvage the timber. Twenty years on when I bought my first boat, John heard I was going to name her *Miss Ruth* after my daughter, and he asked me to call at his builders' yard saying he had something for me. It turned out to be a nicely carved name board from the schooner which I still have today.

August 6. Yacht *Kingfisher*. Saved boat and two persons.

December 22. *MV Vrede* was aground on Lukes Point near Bangor. The weather was squally with rain showers and when the lifeboat came close alongside three crewmen leapt aboard.

The captain and some of the rest of the crew refused to leave even though the engine room was flooded and the ship was pounding on the rocks. After the lifeboat landed the survivors, it returned to the casualty as she was in danger of breaking up, and they stood by for six hours when, by this time, the wind had moderated.

1944

September 3. Only one rescue this year – yacht *Trefoil*. Saved boat and two persons.

1945

January 4. *MV Oregon,* a large vessel of 4,000 tons with a crew of forty two, ran onto rocks at Wilson's Point. When the lifeboat came on the scene, evacuation had already started by Breeches Buoy as the vessel was so close inshore, so they stood by until it was complete. The ship broke her back and the stern half was brought round to Ballyholme Bay and beached, where it was eventually towed away.

January 18. An almost identical grounding happened in the same place to *MV Samanco,* a ship of 8,355 tons with seventy two persons on board. They were landed on shore by the same method with the lifeboat standing by for a few hours.

January 23. A naval vessel was reported to be ashore on Barclay's Rock at Ballyhaskin. When the lifeboat came alongside, the crew were going to abandon their boat as it was taking water, but Coxswain White suggested that they would try to tow them off first. Once they had the tow arranged the boat came off the rock quite easily so they continued up to Donaghadee. As it was nearing high water they were able to berth the casualty in Lemon's Wharf where she would dry out. Saved boat & 10 persons.

July 15. Word came from the Coastguard that people were stranded aboard a yacht in Ballyholme Bay in very heavy sea conditions because of the northerly gale that was blowing. When the lifeboat approached they could see it was the yacht *Dolphin* with five men aboard. The skipper, Mr David Steadman, was a well known and very capable yachtsman. There were very steep seas in the Bay at this time and to transfer the men was very difficult but at last they were able to proceed to Donaghadee to land them.

August 9. Towed to Donaghadee a Naval patrol vessel with engine trouble.

Civil Service No. 5

May 1. Just one call this year, but a big one. *SS Georgetown Victory,* a Ministry of War Transport, with 1,200 persons aboard went ashore on Killard Point, Strangford Lough. Luckily the morning was fine and clear with a very light north east breeze. When *Civil Service* arrived at the scene there were many other boats alongside the casualty and the evacuation was well under way. It was decided that the lifeboat would take the stretcher cases and others. The lifeboat left at 3.30 pm and landed forty two persons. The ship became a total loss.

1946

February 12. Reserve lifeboat on station. A call was received from *SS Sylvafield* that they had a crewman injured and needed a doctor. The ship was anchored in Carrick Roads and had asked for a tug to bring a doctor from Belfast but, with a strong south-easterly wind with heavy snow, it was considered too rough for the tug and so the lifeboat was sent for at 2.30 pm. The boat called into Bangor Harbour, picked up a doctor and proceeded on to Carrick, where the doctor was put aboard the steamer to treat the man's injuries. The lifeboat returned the doctor to Bangor and was on station at 7.30 pm.

1947

Outgoing and incoming coxswains, Andrew White and Hugh Nelson, 1950

April 22. A report came in saying that a Larne fisherman, who had been missing for two days, had been located on one of the Maidens Islands and the lifeboat was needed to bring him ashore. As the coxswain was unsure of the position of the outlying rocks and shoals near the islands he called at Larne where he obtained the help of a local pilot, a Mr Robert Houston, who was well acquainted with the area. The man was seen standing on the rocks and was taken aboard and returned safe and well to Larne. The lifeboat returned to station at 8.15 pm, having been at sea for over six hours.

The awards to the crew for this service was £1:15:0, or in today's money £1.75. The pilot was awarded £1:1:0.

September 11. *Reina Del Pacifico* was on sea trials from Harland & Wolff, sixteen miles north of the Copeland Islands when she had an engine room explosion in which sixty men were badly injured, mostly with burns. Two local doctors, J.F.S. McKee and F.R. Grant boarded the lifeboat which set course for the ship. The wind was light westerly with only a slight swell. After they put the doctors aboard, the ship's captain asked the coxswain if he would stand by as tugs were on their way with doctors, stretchers and medical supplies and would need the lifeboat to transfer them to the ship. This was a massive ship of 27,000 tons with

200 shipyard workers on board. After the doctors and equipment were put aboard, the tugs took the vessel in tow with the lifeboat standing by until they were well into Belfast Lough. The captain then informed the coxswain that the doctors would remain on board until the injured were put ashore in Belfast. The boat returned to station. This was a terrible accident with twenty four dead and thirty four injured.

October 12. Coastguards requested the lifeboat to search around the large Copeland Island for a small sailing boat missing with three persons on board where it had been last seen. After searching for about an hour and not finding anything the coxswain widened the search to include the two outlying islands and, on approaching Mew Island, the lifeboat signalled to the Lighthouse keepers who affirmed that the three men were in the Lighthouse and were safe and well. Next morning they were taken off by a motor boat from Groomsport. There is no mention of the sail boat.

1948

September 15. A schooner was seen to be firing flares approximately one mile off Bangor pier. *Civil Service* launched at 8.55 am and was alongside the *Antelope* about 10.20 am after a rough passage round into Bangor Bay against the northerly gale. After some difficulty the five men were safely aboard and landed in Donaghadee at 11.30 am. At 6.30 pm the same evening another call from the Coastguard relayed that now the gale had abated, the ship was lying in a dangerous place in the way of other shipping. Captain Houston, who was also the schooner's owner, had to be found along with his crew and taken back by lifeboat to their ship.

September 18. Portpatrick Radio had received a report from a trawler *Flanders* that they had picked up two men adrift in a motorboat whose engine had failed. Arrangements were made to rendezvous with the lifeboat two miles off Donaghadee and tow the boat in.

1949

February 23. A request from a Swedish vessel heavily loaded with iron ore bound for Manchester, saying he was anchored in Carrick Roads for shelter and he had two injured men who needed a doctor urgently. Doctor N. F. Kelly was contacted and taken to the ship where he treated their injuries and made them comfortable for their onward voyage.

April 2. *SS Clew Bay* ashore one mile south of Larne Lough; stood by until refloated by tugs.

December 19. Stood by *SS Florence Cooke* aground on Ballymacormick Point loaded with explosives, but refloated at high tide.

1950

March 15. At 3.15 am Coastguards observed red flares being fired approximately five miles east of Orlock Head. When the lifeboat was proceeding to this area they could see the flares were being fired from Mew Island. When they got within signalling range they learned that one of the Lighthouse keepers was either dead or dying. As it was just after low water the lifeboat could not make a landing so they steamed back to Donaghadee Harbour and towed the boarding boat back to the island. The coxswain Hugh Nelson sent four of his crew to the island where they learned of the death of a young keeper, twenty one year old Richard Power, who had only been on the island for three days. He had been drowned after falling into an old gas tank that stored water for cooling the fog horn engines. The Principal Keeper asked the lifeboat men to take the body ashore where it was given into the care of the RUC. The lifeboat was on station again at 8.30 am.

May 27-28. A small yacht *Fair Head* was reported overdue on passage from Bangor to Whitehead. The *Civil Service* launched at 9.40 pm on what was to be her last service and proceeded to Belfast Lough where they searched until 2 am before returning to station.

Arrangements had been made to have two aircraft in the search area from daylight so the lifeboat launched again at 4 am. The two aircraft carried out a very extensive search but no trace was found with the lifeboat returning to station at 8 am. The missing men were John McVea aged twenty three, his brother Derek (17), Val Greer (17) and William Liversage (16).

The McVea boys were nephews of the lifeboat mechanic James Armstrong who, along with coxswain Hugh Nelson and some crew, was away bringing the new lifeboat home.

Civil Service No. 5 was launched on service 80 times and rescued 56 lives 1932 to 1950.

Sir Samuel Kelly

Sir Samuel Kelly

The station's next new boat was *Sir Samuel Kelly* which cost £25,075 and a gift from Lady Mary Kelly of Crawfordsburn in memory of her late husband.

Again the new boat was a Watson design with a forward and after cabin, 240 hp diesel engines and modern electrics. This was the beginning of one era and the end of another because with the retirement of *Civil Service No. 5* also came the retirement of Coxswain Andrew White after thirty two years. His position was filled by Hugh Nelson who, as is revealed later, went on to carry out his duties with great courage and skill. Sadly Hugh died in November 1954. Alexander Nelson was promoted to coxswain and the position of 2nd coxswain was given to John Trimble.

1950

Hugh Nelson,
Coxswain 1950-1954

Sir Samuel Kelly was named in the summer of that year and only one call out was recorded that year and only two the following year.

August 5. Gave assistance to motorboat *Two Sisters*.

November 6. Landed a sick man from *SS Caslon* of London.

1952

July 12. Yacht *Zamorian* was saved and three persons rescued.

The *Kelly*, as she was known by the crew, had started her career very quietly but things were about to change very dramatically.

1953

January 31. A Saturday, a wild day with winds gusting over 100 mph and very heavy snow showers. Donaghadee is a rugby town and the local team was playing Larne that day. Many of the townspeople, including some of the lifeboat crew, were at the match when the news reached them that *Princess Victoria* was in trouble and that lifeboats were needed. Although they knew they were too late, they made for home where they found out just how serious things were.

Princess Victoria was on regular passages from Stranraer to Larne. That

The crew of the *Sir Samuel Kelly* which went to the rescue of the *Princess Victoria* (l-r) Jim Armstrong, Hugh Nelson, Samuel Herron, Hugh Nelson Jnr, Frank Nelson, John Trimble, George Lindsay, Alec Nelson, William Nelson, Sammy Nelson

morning, sailing was delayed to wait for the London train to arrive. After embarking 128 passengers, many of them women and children, with a crew of fifty one, the ship slipped her moorings and pulled away from the pier. The passage down Lough Ryan was uneventful but as they neared Corsewall Point they encountered the full force of this terrible storm which later became known as the Great Storm when it passed down the English coast where it did great damage and onto the continent causing severe flooding in the Netherlands.

About an hour after leaving Stranraer the ship was hit by a massive wave which damaged the stern doors. The crew was dispatched to shore up the doors but to no avail; water continued to pour into the vessel and the draining scuppers could not discharge it quickly enough. Captain Ferguson on the bridge was faced with the terrible dilemma of how to get his crippled ship to safety and, at about 10.45, the first SOS was sent.

The Portpatrick lifeboat was alerted and launched into the gale en route to the last position given, four miles north west of Corsewall Point. This, as it turned out, was not correct as *Princess Victoria* had drifted south

Alexander Nelson,
Coxswain 1954-1959

which meant the *Jeanie Spiers* was heading in the wrong direction and valuable time was lost. A destroyer, *HMS Contest,* was lying in Rothsay Harbour and was asked to make all speed to the area. All this time a very courageous man, Radio Officer David Broadfoot, was staying at his post sending numerous messages.

After hearing the 1 o'clock news coxswain Hugh Nelson and his son, also called Hugh, made their way to the lifeboat house where shortly afterwards the Honorary Secretary, David McKibbin, requested an immediate launch. A few minutes later *Sir Samuel Kelly* was underway with coxswain Hugh Nelson in charge with 2nd coxswain Alex Nelson, crewmen Hugh Nelson junior, brothers Frank and William Nelson, George Lindsay, Samuel Herron and mechanic James Armstrong.

The position given at this time was five miles east of the Copelands. There were a few ships sheltering near Black Head lighthouse which heard the new position and, with the small tanker *Pass of Drumochter* leading, *Lairdsmoor, Orchy* and a trawler *Eastcoates* left their anchorage and headed out to lend their help. Captain Kelly of the *Pass of Drumochter* reckoned to be in the area in about 1 hour. The ships and the Donaghadee lifeboat had spread out to widen the search area when a call came from the *Orchy* that they were seeing debris – lifejackets etc – in the water. Soon after, Captain Kelly's tanker reached the scene and they immediately spotted a ship's lifeboat with a large number of persons aboard. Conditions were so atrocious that to bring the boat alongside, it would have been smashed to pieces so they managed to get rope aboard, but the danger was that the boat could be drawn into the propeller so he asked Donaghadee Lifeboat to come to him. With difficulty Hugh Nelson managed to come alongside the survivors' boat despite the wild motion and quickly got them into the *Kelly*. Another ship's boat was seen to have one man in it and Hugh had to do the same manoeuvre again to save him. The lifeboat continued to search in the poor conditions of flying spray and snow when a raft was seen with one man clinging to it; he was so cold and exhausted that it was very difficult to get him aboard. Sadly that was the last person to be rescued alive by the *Kelly*. The survivors were landed at Donaghadee harbour at about 6 pm and were taken to the Imperial Hotel. The Portpatrick lifeboat arrived at Donaghadee with two survivors after a very long and arduous day. The Donaghadee crew, after a very short rest, were called out again with two extra crew members on board, bowman John Trimble and another Nelson brother, Samuel. This call out was to meet the trawler *Eastcoates* which had one survivor and six bodies aboard; these were also landed in Donaghadee by the *Sir Samuel Kelly*.

At first light next morning which, by the way, dawned fine and clear, *Sir Samuel Kelly* set sail again to search for survivors but sadly none were found. They searched all day and picked up twelve bodies which they again landed at Donaghadee.

For this outstanding service coxswain Hugh Nelson received three awards, the British Empire Medal, RNLI Bronze Medal and the Maud Smith Award for the bravest act of life saving in 1953. He also received the Thanks of the RNLI on Vellum. Portpatrick lifeboat coxswain William McConnell was also awarded the British Empire Medal. Mechanic James Armstrong received the Thanks of the RNLI on Vellum for the excellent work he carried out at sea. The captains of the four ships were awarded the MBE. Radio Officer David Broadfoot was posthumously awarded the George Cross for his devotion to duty in staying at his post to the very end.

August 7 and 8. Overnight search for a small motorboat lost in fog. Saved boat and eight persons.

December 23. *SS Grace Hill* aground on rocks at Mew Island in thick fog. As the tide was rising the captain asked the lifeboat to stay alongside while he assessed if his ship was damaged. The vessel refloated under her own power and continued her passage to Larne.

1954

March 29. At about 6.15 pm Maidens Lighthouse requested the help of the lifeboat to land a sick keeper and also bring a reserve keeper from Ferris Point. It was raining with poor visibility and a strong southerly wind. After embarking the reserve keeper at Larne, the boat proceeded to the island where, with difficulty, the sick man was got on board and the other keeper landed. They made their way back to Larne where the casualty was put ashore at 10.45 pm. Returned to station at 1.30 am.

September 7. Message was received from Maidens Lighthouse that a ship, *SS Overton* of Liverpool, was aground on Saddle Rock near their island and that conditions at the scene were very foggy but calm. The *Sir Samuel Kelly* launched at 6.50 am and proceeded north, arriving at the casualty at 9.30 am, by which time seven of the crew had taken to the boats. The captain, mate, and chief engineer stayed aboard. The crewmen were taken aboard the lifeboat and after some time got back on their own ship.

As the tide was rising the captain had his men remove some of the hatch covers to see if there was any damage down below only to discover seven feet of water in the forward hold and eleven feet in the after hold. He then asked coxswain Alex Nelson to land his crewmen in Larne. Before leaving the ship Coxswain Nelson asked the lighthouse keepers by radio to keep watch as he feared that with the incoming tide the vessel would take on a dangerous list or, worse still, maybe slip off the rock into deeper water. They had only travelled about one mile when a message from the keepers told them the other men had taken to the boats. The lifeboat turned and picked up the three men and their dog. The *Overton* became a total wreck.

November 24. *SS St. Enoch* aground at Muck Island, Co. Antrim. Landed five men in Larne. The vessel was towed off three days later by tugs.

1955

No calls this year.

1956

June 1. Relief lifeboat on station. Motorboat *Seal* was towed in having had engine failure. The boat and four persons were saved.

July 17. Coastguards requested a launch to a ship on the rocks at the Maidens. As *Sir Samuel Kelly* approached they saw the ship, *MV Douglas* of Bergen, was hard and fast on the rocks and there was a ship's lifeboat with five persons in it. They were taken onto the lifeboat, and when they

(l-r) Sammy Nelson, John Trimble, Pat McDowell, Jim Armstrong, Tommy Trimble, Jim Bunting, Hugh Nelson

came alongside the casualty the rest of the crew put all their belongings into the *Kelly*. The captain said his radio had been damaged in the grounding and he requested the coxswain to remain alongside to relay messages.

July 18. An attempt was made to refloat the ship using a tug which proved unsuccessful, and it was decided to jettison the cargo. The captain still insisted the lifeboat stand by but during the night the wind increased and the lifeboat had to lie off within hailing distance.

July 19. The crew once again boarded the lifeboat as number two hold was flooded and water had entered the engine room. A further attempt was made to tow the vessel off, again unsuccessful. The captain then asked for four of his crew to be landed at Larne.

After this was done, the captain of the *Douglas* consulted the captain of the tug and the decision was made to release the lifeboat as the tug was going to stay with the casualty.

The *Sir Samuel Kelly* returned to station at 9 pm after being at sea for sixty hours.

John Trimble,
Coxswain 1959-67

1957   **August 20.** A small rowing boat with two men and a boy was seen to capsize half a mile off Ballywhisken. The lifeboat was called, arriving on scene in about thirty minutes. Another small boat had picked up one man and his grandson but the other man was missing. The lifeboat made a very extensive search and a helicopter was also called in to help but unfortunately nothing was found. A few weeks later Mr Cleland's body was found washed up at the mouth of Loch Ryan.

1958   **March 7.** Gave assistance to motorboat *Whiteheather* which was aground on Mew Island.

July 13. Reserve lifeboat *Edmund and Mary Robinson* saved yacht *Linda* and four persons.

October 18. Lifeboat launched at 6.15 am to *MV Clipper* of Rotterdam aground on Saddle Rock near where the wreck of the *Overton* lay. Things were not so serious this time and the lifeboat stood by until the vessel floated and followed her to Larne.

1959   **June 12.** Coastguards reported that an Admiralty vessel *DCV 400* was on Deputy Reef. There was dense fog that morning and after searching along the reef the lifeboat could find no trace of any vessel. On extending the search area they discovered the ship on Governor Rocks. On going alongside they found that the ship had damaged her rudder and, as it was very calm and the tide was ebbing, they were not in danger but it was going to be a wait of about ten hours before there would be enough water to float her off.

Later that afternoon the lifeboat towed the casualty off the rocks and out into deep water where another naval ship *HMS Barragh* was waiting to tow her to Belfast.

October 5. *Kelly* back on station after a refit and launched at 3.05 am to the aid of fishing vessel *C Risager* of Whitehaven with engine breakdown off Carnlough. Towed the casualty to Larne and returned home at 2.45 pm.

December 19. Trawler *Auk* sending distress signals at Ballymacormick Point. The lifeboat set out at 6 pm and found the vessel hard on the rocks. Luckily the tide was just about to turn so it wasn't long before she floated and was escorted to Bangor Harbour undamaged. The skipper said he had got confused with flashing Christmas tree lights in one of the houses near the point thinking it was the flashing light on Bangor pier head.

This service was the first time the new parachute flares were used and coxswain Alex Nelson said that they were going to be of great benefit in night searches. This was to be Coxswain Nelson's last service in charge. The reins passed over to John Trimble.

1960

July 29. Reports came in of an aircraft crashing in the sea off Black Head. A very wide search area was covered by the lifeboat, many other boats and a helicopter, but only the pilot's helmet and pieces of the plane were found by the lifeboat.

1961

July 5. Two boys stranded on rocks at Millisle were rescued and landed in Donaghadee.

September 14. A call was received from Port Muck Coastguard that a small boat was missing from Larne. The lifeboat left the moorings at 8.30 pm and proceeded northwards to begin the search. After looking round the Maidens and not finding any sign of the casualty they carried on north, eventually finding a small motorboat *Zelda* with her engine broken down so they took her in tow to Larne. They arrived well after midnight to find a Mr Logan, an engineer, on Larne Harbour had arranged with a local hotel to give the crew a meal, which was very gratefully received. On station again 5.30 am.

The reserve lifeboat on station for this call was a very renowned boat, the *Mary Stanford*. This boat was stationed at Ballycotton near Cork and was involved in a very dramatic rescue of the crew of the *Daunt* light vessel which had broken her anchor chain and was adrift in a horrendous storm. The waves washing over the lighthouse were over 200 feet high and tearing stone blocks over a ton weight from the harbour walls. The boat was at sea for three days standing by. Eventually it became too dangerous and the crew had to be taken off with enormous difficulty. For this rescue coxswain Patsy Sliney was awarded RNLI Gold Medal. One was also given to the boat and was framed and mounted in the forward cabin.

December 7. The captain of *MV Durham Brook* radioed ashore saying the ship had an explosion in the engine room and he needed the lifeboat and a doctor as he had a man badly burned. The lifeboat left harbour at 7.20 pm with Dr Graham Ker on board. Dr Ker gave the man first aid and arranged to have him moved to hospital. The lifeboat was back in harbour at 9 pm where the injured man was taken to the waiting ambulance.

1962

June 14. Police in Whitehead reported a fishing boat with three persons on board drifting off Blackhead Lighthouse. At 1.50 am reserve lifeboat *Edward Z Dresden* left her moorings, and on nearing the scene they saw the *Betsy* had eleven fishermen on board, not three. All were very glad to have the lifeboat there as they had been adrift since 9 pm the night before. The lifeboat towed *Betsy* back to Bangor, arriving at 5 am.

August 23. Blackhead Lighthouse reported a small rowing boat in distress one mile south-east of the lighthouse. The occupants were taken on to the lifeboat and their boat towed to Whitehead where they were landed at the pier.

October 1. Landed sick crewman in Bangor from Dutch *MV Holweirde*.

1963

April 20. At 10.10 pm a fire was noticed by the lifeboat mechanic Jim

John and Tommy Trimble

Armstrong on the Large Copeland. This has always been a signal that help is needed. The *Kelly* was launched, towing the boarding boat so that a party could be landed. When we got to the jetty we were told a sixteen year old deaf and dumb boy was very ill and could not walk. We called Belfast Coastguard on VHF Radio who alerted Dr Sargaison to go to Donaghadee Harbour to board the lifeboat to go to the island. After examination by the doctor the boy was placed on a stretcher and carried down the island. The lifeboat arrived back in harbour at 3.25 am.

May 26. Coastguard requested the lifeboat to investigate a light flashing north-east of Orlock Head. When we got to the position we found a small speedboat off Donaghadee. Towed in.

May 16. Speedboat *Jungfrau*, with three adults and one child on board, was firing distress flares; towed to Donaghadee.

1964

June 26. *Zulu Warrior* of Castletown, Isle of Man towed to Donaghadee with engine trouble.

1965

Just one call to assist a fishing boat.

1966

George Lindsay,
Coxswain 1967

1967

April 8. I remember this call very well. It was Grand National day and we got the call just as the race was about to start. It was to a pirate radio ship, *Radio Scotland,* anchored four miles east of Donaghadee. One of the crew had got caught in the chain as they dropped anchor and had lost a finger. We brought the injured man ashore to be taken to hospital.

June 4. Gave assistance to *Sarna* of Bangor.

July 27. Saved power boat and three persons.

December 8. 11.40 pm. Sea Vixen aircraft reported crashed at the entrance of Belfast Lough. The coxswain in charge now was George Lindsay, John Trimble having retired. There were quite a number of boats searching when we arrived with two aircraft scanning the area but all we picked up was some wreckage and the pilot's seat. The search was called off around midnight and we returned to Donaghadee. It was arranged that we would return to the scene at 6.30 am next morning. After combing the area all day nothing else was found and the search was called off at 7.30 pm.

Sadly not long after this call coxswain George Lindsay died suddenly and 2nd coxswain Jim Bunting took over.

Jim Bunting,
Coxswain 1967-1983

August 17 and 18. Red flares were reported being fired at the entrance to Belfast Lough. *Sir Samuel Kelly* was launched at 11 pm. On reaching the scene a search was started, eventually finding a small dinghy with two foreign students in it who had been fishing near John's Island and had got swept away with the strong tide. The lifeboat delivered them back to the island safe and well.

1968

March 9. Another call to John's Island, this time to bring a party of birdwatchers to shore as there was a gale blowing for several days and there was concern about their stock of food. Some of the party were also elderly.

1969

July 28. At 6.15 am a message was received from *MV Partington* saying they had picked up a motor launch *Annie Watterson* in mid channel with three persons on board. They arranged to meet off Donaghadee and for the lifeboat to tow the casualty in to harbour.

March 28. Flares were seen four miles north of Orlock Head. It was a very squally day with heavy rain and a force seven north-westerly wind, and when we arrived on scene we were faced with a massive ex-Navy wooden trawler rolling very violently. It was quite a struggle for the crew

1970

John Trimble, George Lindsay and Alec Nelson

to make their way to the bow of the vessel to make the tow rope fast. It was a slow pull to Donaghadee. Saved boat and three persons.

May 30. Saved small motorboat and three persons.

September 9. Towed in cabin cruiser.

1971   **April 24 and 25.** Reserve lifeboat *Michael Stephens* launched at 9.45 am to continue the search for three men who had been coming ashore from their yacht at Cultra when their dinghy overturned. Bangor inshore lifeboat had picked up one survivor but had to return to station because of darkness. Many boats from the Royal North of Ireland Yacht Club helped in the search but unfortunately nothing was found.

1972   **January 11.** An urgent request for the lifeboat came from Mew Island Lighthouse saying they had a man injured and needed him brought ashore as soon as possible. 2nd coxswain Jack Simpson was in charge and when he assessed the keeper's severe head injuries he decided not to move him. He called the Coastguard to have a doctor brought out by helicopter who had him airlifted to hospital.

March 2. A Greek tanker *Maria Venizolos* had a badly injured man on board. The lifeboat made contact with the tanker off Donaghadee and brought the man to the harbour to be taken to hospital by ambulance. The injured man was Alexander Pezonis and he had suffered broken ribs and a fractured skull.

April 30. Small coaster *Schiestroom* in danger of being blown ashore after her engine failed near Orlock Head. Towed to Bangor Harbour. Saved boat and four persons.

1973

May 12. Converted fishing boat *Uberous* from Portpatrick in difficulties; towed to Donaghadee.

May 16. Again *Uberous,* this time ashore in Whitehead Bay, so close in the crew was able to scramble onto the outer wall of the town's swimming pool. The boat became a total loss.

June 5. Angling boat *Sarna* in difficulties. Stood by and gave help.

1974

Nelsons of Donaghadee

The *Sir Samuel Kelly* and *Nelsons of Donaghadee*

A new concept of lifeboat design, a fast semi-planning hull used by the American Coastguard costing £200,000, was introduced to the RNLI at the end of the 1960s and it was decided to station one of these boats at Donaghadee. The new boat was to be named *Nelsons of Donaghadee* in recognition of the contribution the Nelson families had made to lifesaving in Donaghadee. During a trip home from Poole after engine repairs with Inspector Tony Course, coxswain Jim Bunting, mechanic Walker Simpson and the crew were involved in a very rough passage and it was the weekend of the ill-fated Fastnet Race when a large number of yachts and yachtsmen were lost. Unfortunately, with having prolonged engine

1976

Walker Simpson,
Lifeboat Mechanic

problems, the *Nelsons* was only used on one service that was an all night search for a fishing boat, *The Robert Charles,* with one man aboard resulting in towing it to Peel on the Isle of Man. The lifeboat performed very well but later was still plagued by engine trouble and had to be replaced by relief boats including *Sir Samuel Kelly.*

Unfortunately the records for 1977 and 1978 have been misplaced, so details for these years remain sketchy.

Donaghadee Lifeboat

Arthur and Blanche Harris

Arthur and Blanche Harris

Eventually in 1979 the *Nelsons* was replaced by a similar vessel, *Arthur and Blanche Harris,* and in 1983 coxswain Jim Bunting retired and I, William Lennon, took over as coxswain.

1979

September 2. My first call as coxswain was to 30 ft yacht *Heather of Mourne.* It was about eight miles to the casualty and it was blowing south-east force 8 with a fairly lumpy, confused sea. I thought to myself as we pounded our way south that this was all I needed for my first

1983

William Lennon,
Coxswain 1983-1991

shout. A message from the Coastguard told us a crewman aboard the yacht had sustained a severe head injury on being struck by the boom. As we approached the yacht, it was fairly obvious that it was going to be extremely difficult to transfer the patient to the lifeboat as both boats were rolling violently. As the patient was unconscious and unable to help himself the skipper and I decided that it would be better for us to stand by them to Donaghadee. An ambulance was waiting to take him to hospital where he was found to have a fractured skull. A few weeks later I received a very nice letter from him thanking the crew.

During the next few weeks we had a spate of hoax calls and much time and fuel was wasted on fruitless searches for red flares.

December 9. At 4.30 am I was awakened by the telephone and immediately could hear the wind screeching. An English voice on the line suggested it was going to be a nice morning for a sail. I recognised it to be a friend of mine, Stephen Palmer, a local Coastguard who, I thought being on all night watch, was pulling my leg because it was such a bad night. He assured me it was no joke and that a Naval ship was in difficulties near Ballyferris Point.

With no engine power he said the wind was north north-east at over 50 knots, a force 10. I knew that with that amount of wind and from that direction it would not be long before she would be driven ashore so all haste was made to assemble the crew. The Honorary Secretary and I decided not to fire the maroons but to telephone who we thought would be the most experienced for such conditions. We launched with myself, 2nd coxswain Quinton Nelson, mechanic Walker Simpson, crewmen Gerald Nelson, John McGimpsey, and Graham McConnell.

The passage southwards to the casualty wasn't too bad as we were running before the large following sea. When we got there we discovered that as well as the ship's crew there were thirty Marines aboard. The officer in charge told us he had organised with his base in Belfast for helicopters to airlift the men off, but as we both could see there wasn't going to be time because of her drift towards the lee shore, which by now she was about half a mile off. To give ourselves some time we connected a tow line and, with the Waveney lifeboat straining every horse power, we inched very slowly off shore. Then three helicopters arrived on scene but winching was greatly hampered by the wild pitching of the boats, although we were still managing to keep the casualty head to wind. Then when about half the Marines were lifted away, I had a call on VHF radio from two large Portavogie trawlers on passage home from Campbelltown in Scotland asking if they could assist us. I told them we were having a struggle trying to hold her off, and they said they were about 10 miles away and could be with us in about an hour. This was good news as we were only just holding our own.

As the winching continued the lieutenant in charge decided to send some of his boat's crew ashore in the helicopters as he could now see the trawlers in the distance. He kept three men aboard to ready the ship for the new tow. When the trawlers were in position we passed our tow line to the first boat and, as the lifeboat was the more manoeuvrable, we went close to *Vigilant* and connected another towrope to the other fishing boat. Then started a slow and very bumpy trip northwards to Donaghadee Sound where by this time the seas were even more vicious as the tide now was running into the teeth of the gale making progress even slower. Once we got to the middle of Belfast Lough there was a dramatic improvement. As we had been at sea for eight hours we decided with the Coastguard that we should break off temporarily to get some food which our wives brought to Bangor Harbour – some soup and sandwiches which were very gratefully received. Just as we were finishing our meal we had a call from the Coastguard that one of the cross channel ferries, *Antrim Princess*, was in difficulties at Muck Island on the Antrim Coast.

So once again we got under way set a course for the new casualty after

Crew of the Arthur and Blanche Harris: Front row (l-r): Willie Lennon, Walker Simpson, Morton McAuley, Jim Bunting,. Middle row (l-r): Alistair McKinney, Head Coastguard Bill Mills, Henry Vandenburg. Back row (l-r): Bill Sherrard, Alan Finlay, John McAuley, Billy Gilmour

being assured *Vigilant* was in no further danger and the tow was going well. When we were abeam of Black Head Lighthouse we began to feel the strength of the storm again and soon we could see *Antrim Princess* pitching and rolling violently with no sign of the fire which had disabled her. She had both anchors down and now seemed to be holding although she was only three hundred yards from the cliffs. We could see that to try and get passengers through the gangway doors in the ship's side would be impossible as these doors were sometimes under water as the ship rolled. The Master of the vessel, Captain Cree, called us on VHF radio that another ferry was going to attempt to tow them to Larne. In the mean-time, Belfast Coastguard was organising helicopters much to our relief, as I just couldn't see how we were going to disembark hundreds of pas-sengers and crew as it would soon be dark and conditions were horrible. Then suddenly, just as the other ferry fired a rocket line to the *Antrim Princess,* a helicopter appeared overhead and, whether it was the storm or the draft from the chopper, the rocket shot upwards and fouled the rotor blades of the helicopter. With a lot of skill and a fair bit of luck the pilot managed to coax his aircraft over the cliffs and land on Larne golf course to disentangle the line. By this time the Coastguard had got hold of seven or eight more helicopters, some from Scotland, and soon real shuttle service was in progress. As we watched we couldn't help wondering what was going through some of these elderly ladies' minds as they swung on the end of a very thin wire. We were having a fairly miserable time being tossed about in a small lifeboat but we wouldn't have traded places with people on *Antrim Princess*. We were also full of admiration for the helicopter crews as they fought their aircraft against the wind and had to avoid masts etcetera as well as a very pronounced heaving deck.

It was now getting dark and still the airlift continued and we were joined by a very large steel trawler who hove to about a half mile to seaward but didn't join in any of the very busy VHF chatter. An hour or so later we had another welcome addition to our small fleet, a very large tug sent from the Clyde to help. By this time the passengers had all been evacuated and we were still standing by for the crew, with conditions still very bad. My crew and I were feeling the strain of being tossed about for fourteen hours, so when the Coastguard suggested that since the tug was not intending to attempt to tow the *Antrim Princess* until first light in the morning, we could be released for a few hours as the tug was going to stand by. We left the scene and made our way to Larne Harbour where we were met by members of the local lifeboat committee and arrangements were made for us in Curran Court Hotel where we had a great meal and a place to rest.

The call came for us to go to sea again about 3.30 and so we were off again. The weather was much the same as we had left it and we took up our position again and waited for things to happen with the tug. Just as dawn was breaking the wind started to moderate so things began to happen; the tug men got their ropes made fast to the *Antrim Princess* and slowly took up the strain as the ship's anchors were winched in. The tug headed off the coast to have some sea room then gently turned to starboard with us following behind. After some time we got near to the Channel buoys and calm water, the first we had seen in two days. We were released by the Coastguard and headed for home twenty six hours after leaving Donaghadee.

February 5. Small inflatable dinghy off Groomsport: saved boat and three persons.

May 27. A small passenger launch *Bangor Crest* ran ashore on Ballyma-

1984

cormick Point with a party of anglers aboard who were able to scramble ashore on to the rocks to safety.

The three crew members stayed aboard, and were towed off into deeper water by another motor boat, discovering just as we arrived in the life-boat that *Bangor Crest* was holed and was filling rapidly. We drew alongside just as she was settling down. We took the crew off and took up the tow. With the greater power we were able to make *Bangor Crest* plane up to the surface, enabling us to get her to Groomsport and beach her in the harbour mouth.

The records for the next two years have been mislaid so the details are only from the service boards and my memory.

June 5. Cruiser *Same Again.* Saved boat and 2 persons.

June 8. Gave help to speedboat *Slo Mo Shun.*

June 10. Yacht *Caliban* suffered an engine break down; towed to Groomsport.

July 1. Saved yacht *Fiver* of Howth and four persons.

The next few weeks were very foggy and we were kept busy.

July 8. Motor cruiser *Major B* and yacht *Vicky* left Strangford on passage to the west coast of Scotland in thick fog. After being underway for about an hour they lost their bearings and decided to anchor. Sometime later the fog lifted slightly and to their alarm they discovered they were surrounded by rocks. We launched and proceeded southward not knowing exactly where the casualties were but assuming they must be between Southrock lightvessel and Portavogie harbour. They were transmitting on VHF radio every five minutes so we could track them on our direction finder and eventually we found them indeed ringed by angry-looking rocks. How they got in there without touching anything seemed impossible, but after several attempts with our echo sounder going, we found a deep enough path to lead the two boats out and escort them to Donaghadee.

July 11. *MV Miss Donna,* three persons aboard. Lost in the fog and with engine trouble. Towed to Donaghadee.

July 14. Speedboat *Georgian.* three persons aboard. Lost in the fog, towed to Donaghadee.

July 19. Belfast Coastguard reported a distress call from *MV Star of Down* saying they had left Peel, Isle of Man, for Belfast that morning and were

Arthur and Blanche Harris takes part in a helicopter training exercise

completely lost. Peel lifeboat and Portpatrick lifeboat were launched and, as they were not fitted yet with the new direction finders, we were asked to launch too. After we left harbour we contacted the casualty and asked him to keep up the usual call every five minutes for our direction finder to be able to home on him. We were getting his transmission quite weakly but the other lifeboats were getting him strong; his bearing from us was due east so we reckoned he must be near the Mull of Galloway. We were gradually getting his signal more strongly, so we slowed down and I asked him if he had a radar reflector, which he said he had. On our radar we could we could see two targets which we believed to be the two lifeboats, then out of the fog appeared *Star of Down* with the skipper standing on the deck holding up a grill pan as a reflector. We took them under tow to Portpatrick. Four persons aboard.

July 21. *Miss Donna* again in fog towed to Donaghadee. Three persons aboard.

July 30. *Maid of Berrow* with five on board, towed to Donaghadee.

August 4. Liverpool ferry *Saint Colum* required help with an ill woman on board. We launched with my daughter Ruth who was then a nurse on her first service. We were glad to have a woman with us, as I'm sure the patient was too, as she had suffered a miscarriage and would not have wanted six big lifeboatmen dealing with her.

Arthur and Blanche Harris puts to sea

August 15. Gave assistance to *MV Nordica* of Sweden.

August 26. Gave assistance to yacht *Spray*.

October 24. We got a call to go to the aid of eight birdwatchers marooned on Old Lighthouse Island for several days with their food running low. Landed safely in Donaghadee.

1985

February 1. Another call from *Saint Colum* on passage to Liverpool. Landed sick woman to waiting ambulance in Donaghadee.

February 12. Brought sick lighthouse keeper from Mew Island to Donaghadee harbour.

Arthur and Blanche Harris was previously stationed at Barry Dock in Wales where she rescued 57 lives and, in her period in Donaghadee, she was launched on service 81 times and rescued 41 lives. During this period relief boats on station launched 11 times and saved 1 life.

City of Belfast

City of Belfast
Photograph courtesy of Rick Tomlinson

In 1984-85 the Station Secretary Bill Sherrard and I arranged a meeting with the Lord Mayor of Belfast. Mr Alfie Ferguson was a keen fisherman and a personal friend of mine who had a view to raising an appeal to provide an Arun class lifeboat for Donaghadee. He was most helpful and keen to do what he could. The cost of the Arun, £433,138, was met by the appeal and other legacies. The name of our Arun was to be *City of Belfast* as a mark of respect to the generosity of Belfast and Northern Ireland public.

In mid November 1985 half of our crew and I were asked to go to Poole

1985

City of Belfast arrives in Donaghadee

in Dorset for training in the new boat and the rest of the crew stayed at home to keep the station open. The mornings were spent in the classroom, the afternoons at sea. The training went very well indeed.

Then on handover day we were to go to Moody's Boatyard on the Hamble River to have some adjustments to the trim tabs done before staying overnight in Weymouth. Just as we were about to leave I discovered we had thirteen on board and no way could I sail in a new boat with that number aboard. David Martin and John McGimpsey opted to go to Weymouth by bus. We left Weymouth about 4 am on very frosty morning with just a slight breeze on passage to St. Peter Port in the Channel Islands. Sailing with us were Dr Richard Bryans and lifeboat inspector for Ireland Jeff Mankertz.

About three hours into our trip we received a message from St. Peter Port Coastguard that a fishing boat was making water and needed help. His position was fourteen miles from Guernsey and about five miles from us. We were a bit dubious at first, thinking it was arranged by the inspector, but he assured us it was genuine. When we arrived on scene the *Azkarra* was low in the water. We stood by and eventually her own pumps were able to clear the water, the crew were able to fix the broken pipe which was the cause of their trouble and they continued on their way.

Almost immediately the Coastguard called us again saying another fishing vessel had lost its rudder and was out of control, this one was about seven miles away from us. This *City of Belfast* seemed as if it was going to

Willie Lennon welcomes the Duke
of Kent on board

be a very busy lifeboat; two calls and this only the second day.

We soon came upon *Our Matthew*, rudderless and with crab pots piled high on her decks. The skipper gave me the Decca co-ordinates. He wanted me to tow him along as he wanted to shoot the pots. This he did and we towed him the remaining six miles to St. Peter Port Harbour, arriving at 11.30 am.

A very eventful delivery passage with 200 gallons used.

November 24. The passage from St. Peter Port to Newlyn was covered in eight hours thirty minutes and nothing of note happened until we reached Newlyn Harbour where we discovered the port engine would not slow down. This is not a great situation to be in with the harbour wall approaching at eighteen knots, but we managed to turn the boat and stop the port engine, entering Newlyn under control with one engine. We had to spend two days here undergoing repairs to the engine. During our stay we paid a visit to Penlee lifeboat house where the ill-fated *Solomon Brown* left on her last call. It was a very moving experience to see the way it had been left as if to await the crew's return.

November 27. We had four hours of engine trials which were satisfactory so it was decided that we would do a night passage to Rosslare to make up the lost time as we were due in Donaghadee on Sat 30th. This was a fairly bumpy trip round Lands End and across the Channel as the

City of Belfast in her new home

wind was on our nose the whole way across. After our nine hour trip we refuelled with 450 gallons. We then carried on up the Irish Coast to Wicklow where the inspector lived. We stayed the night here and were very well looked after by the Wicklow crew in the local yacht club. The plan was to go to Portpatrick next morning to be convenient to home for Saturday. When some of the local crew heard we were landing in Scotland they asked if they could get a lift with us as they were going to attend the funeral in Scotland of very well-known lifeboatman Tom Beattie. Next morning we were all assembled on the pier when I noticed there were thirteen again. Coxswain Reuben Dover said that it would not be a problem, disappearing up the town and arriving back very soon with another man who still sends me Christmas cards signed *'the four-teenth man'*. The passage north was beautiful, bright sunshine and calm sea lasting seven and a half hours using 350 gallons.

Portpatrick being our nearest offshore lifeboat neighbours, the crew are well known to us. The coxswain, Robert Erskine, worked with me on my trawler for years so it was just like bringing a new boat home to our own station. We were so well received, wined and dined, and it turned out to be a long night.

November 30. The big day dawned bright and clear which could not be said for the lifeboatmen. We refuelled, dressed the boat overall and set off for Donaghadee. The weather by this time had changed, the wind was strong south-easterly with a very rough sea. We were met by coxswain Gerry McLaughlin with the rest of our crew in the station Waveney lifeboat, *Arthur and Blanche Harris,* just north of the Copeland Islands and, as they were escorting us down the Sound, we were met by a very old lifeboat owned by Mr Ray Woods. The harbour walls were lined with people who later told us how impressive the *City of Belfast* looked in the rough conditions. This was one of my proudest moments, when I brought *City of Belfast* through the pier heads in Donaghadee.

The next two weeks were taken up by very intense crew training to familiarise the crewmen, who were not on the delivery trip, with all the new equipment.

November 11. Just four days after being handed over to the station *City of Belfast* got her first Donaghadee call to a Greek vessel in Belfast Lough to a seaman suffering severe abdominal pain. He was transferred to ambulance in Bangor. We later heard he had appendicitis.

1986

January 8. Another medical call, this time to a Yugoslav grain carrier *Sebanic.* A sailor had fallen from the main deck into the hold, a depth of over twenty five feet. This ship was empty and when the lifeboat was alongside it was towering above us. It was a very long daunting climb up a rope ladder that faced Dr Richard Bryans and my daughter Ruth who is a paramedic. After the doctor examined the patient he wanted him taken ashore as quickly as possible as his injuries were very serious. We carefully lowered him into the lifeboat and steamed full speed to the harbour to the waiting ambulance. The patient was kept in intensive care for three weeks and several weeks in a main ward before being flown home. This was one life *City of Belfast* definitely saved that night; the doctor said that it was the speed of getting the man to hospital which saved his life.

February 7. At 4.50 am a distress call was received by the Coastguard from a German coaster *Ansbach* saying the ship was aground on the North Rock off Portavogie and was making water rapidly. *City of Belfast* was launched and on the way to the casualty we made our salvage pump ready to hand over. Weather conditions were quite good at the time; the wind was east north-easterly, about force four with a moderate swell, but it was very dark. When we tied up alongside we could see the ship was leaking in the engine room. We got our pump aboard and two of the lifeboatmen stayed to operate it. After a couple of hours the water level was well lowered and our pump seemed able to handle it. We now had to wait for the tide to rise to see if the vessel would refloat. Later in the morning the captain made arrangements with two Portavogie trawlers to tow his vessel at high water, so we stood by until the attempt was made at about midday. When the fishing boats took up the strain, *Ansbach,* after a few groans and creaks, slipped off into deep water. The captain asked us to stay with him as he was unsure of how much damage was done. When the tow had been underway for about an hour the water was seen to be rising again in the engine room and our pump was not holding it. We asked the Coastguard if they could locate another pump, which they were able to do quite quickly and they had it flown out to the ship by helicopter, and not a bit too soon because by this time the stern of the ship was down to deck level. The extra pump made all the difference and we were able to get *Ansbach* on up Belfast Lough to a dry dock in Belfast without further drama, returning to station at 5 pm.

March 20. 6.25 pm. We launched to help a Bulgarian factory ship named *Kondor* which had an injured crewman. The skipper had first contacted the Coastguard a few hours earlier when they were well off the Northern Ireland coast, but he felt it would be easier to transfer the patient in more sheltered waters. We arranged a rendezvous off Glenarm which was sheltered from the strong north-westerly wind. When we had the casualty aboard we found he had fallen through a glass door and had sustained a number of severe lacerations. Just as we were about to leave the ship the skipper asked me if we would pilot his ship to a safe anchorage as he had no charts of the area. I suggested that he drop anchor where he was and after we landed his crewman in Larne we would return and guide him into a Belfast Lough anchorage which we did, returning to station at midnight.

During this six month period the *City of Belfast* was kept very busy with crew training and fund-raising events.

May 2. Distress message received from yacht *Lorne* that due to the bad visibility he did not know his position and he was worried that he could be getting close to the Copeland Islands. The lifeboat was launched at 11.40 pm. The wind was northerly force 5 with choppy sea conditions. After we cleared the harbour we contacted the yacht on VHF radio and asked him if he would give us a 10 second call every 10 minutes so we could home in on him with our direction finder. As it turned out he was about two miles north of the islands, so we escorted the yacht to Carrickfergus.

May 17. Towed to Bangor yacht *Dalriada* which had dismasted mid channel with five crew aboard. Saved yacht and five persons.

May 18. Small 8 foot dinghy with five persons on board was in difficulties a mile off Donaghadee harbour; the lifeboat brought it in and landed.

May 21. Message from Belfast Coastguard that yacht *Rum Runner* was in trouble about eight miles out in the channel. On arrival at the casualty we found she was leaking badly; we loaded our salvage pump aboard and commenced the tow to Bangor Marina.

May 24. This was the day of the naming ceremony for *City of Belfast*. It turned out to be a bright sunny day; we had a very large crowd seated on the pier with a band playing and a lot of RNLI officials from Headquarters. The Lord Mayor of Belfast christened the lifeboat which we had dressed overall. Just after the ceremony was over a helicopter arrived and we went to sea with the Lord Mayor and dignitaries to put the boat through her paces.

July 11. The next call was at night. A speedboat was reported to Belfast Coastguard as being overdue on a trip from Portpatrick to Carrickfergus. The lifeboat launched and we started our search using radar and direction finder. After about an hour's searching we came upon a speedboat, *Blackhawk,* with six persons aboard. The boat had an engine breakdown so we took the people into the lifeboat and took the boat in tow, landing them in Carrickfergus.

August 21. A report reached Belfast Coastguard that a small lobster boat with two men on board was drifting towards rocks between Ballywalter and Ballyhalbert. In the half hour it took us to reach the casualty they had grounded on the rocks. The water was too shallow for us to get near so we had to fire one of our speedlines to the vessel to enable us to get our towrope to them. When we got into deeper water we found the boat had a fouled propeller but the hull was undamaged so we towed the boat to Ballyhalbert harbour.

August 24. Speedboat *Tara Lee* suffered an engine breakdown six miles out with three persons on board. Towed into Donaghadee harbour.

September 21. Belfast Coastguard received a radio message from mo-

City of Belfast tows a stricken fishing vessel

tor cruiser *Dark Huntress* en route from Portpatrick to Donaghadee that she was leaking badly and in danger of sinking two miles east of Mew Island.

When *City of Belfast* approached we could see there were two people aboard and the vessel was very low in the water. We had our salvage pump ready and after getting the boat's crew into the lifeboat, we started pumping immediately. We then towed the boat to Donaghadee.

October 3. A message was received from yacht *Dundrum* adrift six miles due east of South Rock lightvessel and making water. When the lifeboat came alongside we transferred our pump aboard the yacht and commenced the tow to Donaghadee harbour.

October 5. Yacht *Solitaire* ashore on rocks near Millisle; we towed her off and brought her to Donaghadee.

October 7. Fishing vessel *Golden Bough* sustained an engine breakdown east of South Rock lightvessel so was towed to Portavogie, three persons aboard.

October 20. An urgent message came in to Belfast Coastguard from fishing vessel *Stardust* with four men on board. The caller was the man who had steered the boat to the fishing grounds but when it was time to rouse the crew he found to his horror that all the men seemed to be unconscious. The lifeboat crew was assembled at 5.30 am and as soon as Dr Richard Bryans came on board we set off for the casualty. The position given was seven miles south west of Sanda Island off the Mull of Kintyre which was over thirty miles away. When we neared the scene we could see a large Royal Navy ship lying beside two fishing boats. When the doctor went on board *Stardust* he found two men unconscious and, sadly, 1 dead. It was decided by the doctor to have one man transferred to the Navy ship to be taken to hospital in Scotland as soon as possible, and the other two men and the body were brought into the lifeboat. The other fishing boat put two of their crew into *Stardust* to bring it back to Portavogie.

The cause of this tragedy was due to a very frosty night; the men had closed the hatch fully and the gas heater had used up all the oxygen.

November 13. Belfast Coastguard alerted the lifeboat to Scottish fishing boat, *Ros Argus,* of Kircudbright which had a fouled propeller some seven miles from Donaghadee. The vessel was towed to Donaghadee harbour with five crew aboard.

November 24. Distress call heard from *FV Jean Francis* of Whitehaven with one man on board adrift thirteen miles north of Mew Island Lighthouse. Taken in tow to Bangor harbour.

December 9. Landed a sick man suffering a suspected heart attack to a waiting ambulance from Liverpool ferry *St. Colum.*

1986

1986 was a busy year with 27 rescues, 18 lives saved and four persons landed. Approximate value of property saved £420,500. No further details are known.

1987

April 26. A large cabin cruiser, *Carolina,* suffered engine failure several miles east of Copeland Island. Towed to Donaghadee Harbour.

May 2. Yacht *The Brothers* in trouble with sail failure owing to gale force winds seven miles east of Donaghadee. Towed to harbour.

June 3. Belfast Coastguard received a message from *Ionic Ferry* en route from Stranraer to Larne informing them that the ship was aground at the entrance to Larne Harbour with a full load of commercial vehicles and drivers onboard. *City of Belfast* was launched at once and proceeded to Larne where, on arrival, we saw the ferry was high and dry and, as the tide was going out, no attempt could be made to refloat her for at least twelve hours. There was nothing we could do in the mean time, only stand by. At low water we brought out some surveyors to examine the vessel's hull which was undamaged and she floated again at high water unaided.

June 6. Cabin cruiser *Viking* was in a sinking condition with four persons on board twenty four miles from our station. When we got alongside, we found the occupants very distressed and cold so we brought them into the lifeboat. We got our salvage pump going and soon had the water out, then we started the long slow tow back to Donaghadee which took almost seven hours.

August 2. Cabin cruiser in difficulties 10 miles away, saved boat and four persons.

August 3. Capsized dinghy. Saved boat and three persons.

In August and September we had a spate of nine hoax calls which are most frustrating and annoying as they have to be answered and tie up the services of the lifeboat and Coastguard for long hours when there may be a genuine incident.

1988

January 8. A south-east gale was blowing with heavy rain squalls when we were alerted by Belfast Coastguard to an immediate launch to go to the aid of a large fishing vessel which had fouled the propeller with their nets.

The position we were given was five miles south-west of the Mull of Galloway, about sixteen miles from Donaghadee but directly into the teeth of the gale. As it was such a bad day the Coastguard decided to ask Portpatrick lifeboat to launch as well. After a bumpy ride of 1 hour 20 minutes we arrived at the scene. The casualty was an extremely large trawler called *Dumnonia* and, as she was lying broadside, she was rolling alarmingly right over to her beam ends, the seas were breaking over the vessel and to add to the hazards, parts of the net was floating out on the windward side. We asked the skipper if he could position two men up in the bow to take our towrope and after a few minutes two men managed to make their way up the heaving deck. We were ready to try to connect the tow. After a couple of attempts we managed to get a heaving line aboard and soon the fishermen had our heavy nylon towrope pulled on board and connected. *Dumnonia* was very heavy to get underway with so much of her net in the water acting as a sea anchor. A short time later Portpatrick lifeboat came on the scene and the coxswain, Robert Erskine, a good friend of mine, asked what our intentions were. After a bit of a conference Robert and I decided not to tow with the two lifeboats as it was too dangerous in the conditions at that time with the casualty surging and rolling so violently. We also decided to make for Loch Ryan as Portpatrick Harbour entrance would have been too difficult.

After towing for about an hour there was a very loud crack and our towrope parted. Portpatrick boat then secured her tow and carried on. This seemed to be a pattern – each towrope lasted about an hour – so we alternated for the eight hours it took to reach the comparative shelter of Corsewall Point, by which time neither lifeboat had any ropes left without knots. The rest of the journey up Loch Ryan was uneventful and *Dumnonia* was berthed at the ferry pier to await divers. The lifeboats were at sea for thirteen hours and saved the boat and five persons.

July 2. A distress call was received from fishing vessel *Falken* saying she had struck the Hunter Rock near Larne and was damaged and making water. As the casualty was seventeen miles away from Donaghadee we asked if his condition would allow us to get to his position as it would take us an hour to get there. The skipper told that his pumps seemed to be able to keep the water under control and that he did not want to go to Larne as he was booked for a slipway in Portavogie. We then arranged for him to continue on toward Donaghadee, and we met him near Black Head Lighthouse where we transferred our salvage pump and two of our crew to *Falken* and continued to escort the casualty to Portavogie where the slipway was ready to take the casualty out of the water.

On the same day, a most unusual call was received by Belfast Coastguard from the yacht *Dalriada* which was in difficulties thirty miles away after a submarine had surfaced under her, lifting her bodily out of the water and knocking her over on her side. The yacht was crewed by two men and their daughters who had been in bed at time of the collision. One of the girls had been thrown out of her bunk and had suffered quite a bit of bruising.

It took us about one and a half hours to reach the scene to discover the submarine had left and had been replaced by a large Naval vessel *Battleaxe*. The yacht had sunk by the time we arrived but the crew were safe aboard *Battleaxe*, being looked after by the ship's doctor. Eventually

City of Belfast cuts a powerful sight as she slices through the waves
Photograph courtesy of Rick Tomlinson

they were fit enough to board the lifeboat and we landed them at Larne harbour.

July 10. At just after midnight *City of Belfast*, Bangor and Red Bay lifeboats were launched to search for an overdue cabin cruiser with three persons on board. A very large area was to be searched as it was not known where this boat had been bound for.

At 2.15 am on the same night while we were on the previous call, a radio message came through from the Coastguard saying that a young man had fallen down a cliff on Muck Island. By this time the wind had increased to force 6-7 with a very choppy sea and heavy rain. There was no landing place for the lifeboat so we approached the sheltered end of the island and launched our small inflatable Y-boat crewed by George Thompson, Ruth Lennon and Shane McNamara. Armed with torches, medical bag, a stretcher and a VHF radio, they set off for the long climb to the casualty.

On examination Ruth, with her nurse's training, decided that it would be too dangerous to carry the man down the cliff so she asked for a helicopter lift. In hospital it was found he had suffered some broken ribs, a collapsed lung, cracked pelvis and much bruising. It certainly seemed Ruth's assessment had been correct in not trying to get this man to the lifeboat as the carry down the cliff could have killed him.

I would like to add my thanks and praise to the Y-boat crew for a job well done in horrible slippery conditions, especially with Ruth being afraid of heights. We recovered the Y-boat and crew, and then had to make our way back to the search area as the other casualty hadn't been located. It was still raining very hard but now dawn was breaking and a helicopter was brought into the search.

After about an hour the helicopter spotted the casualty and directed us to his position. We found three extremely wet and cold people who were very glad to board the lifeboat. We then made our way to Groomsport towing the cruiser.

July 27. Launched to a yacht reported on the rocks at Orlock Head. We were assisted by Bangor inshore lifeboat and managed to tow the yacht off. We then escorted them to Carrickfergus Marina.

August 20. Report from Belfast Coastguard for an immediate launch to go to the aid of a motor cruiser adrift in mid channel with two adults and three children on board in deteriorating weather conditions. Towed the casualty back to Donaghadee Harbour.

August 21. At 3.45 am *City of Belfast* left her moorings to answer a distress call from yacht *Isabell* with two persons aboard reported to be firing red flares. The position given was twenty six miles south-east of Donaghadee and the weather at the time was a north-west wind just reaching gale force with a sea state rough with five foot swells. As this position was almost at the edge of our area we arrived at the casualty at 5.30 am to find that *Isabell* had steering failure. It was decided to make for Strangford Lough with the yacht under tow. Three hours later Portaferry was reached and the yacht safely berthed. The lifeboat crew was asked ashore for hot drinks and food and while this was taking place *Isabell* slipped away unnoticed and continued on her journey.

September 7. Launched to assist a lone yachtsman reported to be disorientated and unsure of his position. After a two hour search yacht *Endeavour* was found about twenty miles south-east of the station. Towed to Portpatrick.

September 11. Report received that a small boat was in difficulty with two people aboard, the position given was two miles east of Ballywalter. Thirty minutes later we were alongside the casualty to find they had an engine breakdown. We towed the vessel to outside Ballywalter harbour and, as it was too shallow for us, the Coastguard arranged for a small local boat to meet us.

September 18. Casualty firing red flares as they had no radio. As the Honorary Secretary was unavailable and the coxswain was in hospital, a call was received by the 2nd coxswain Graham McConnell who initiated the launch. The lifeboat located the casualty off the coast at Millisle, took the two men into the lifeboat and towed the boat to Donaghadee.

October 13. A request from coaster *Robert M* for a doctor to examine a crewman suffering severe abdominal pain. Dr Richard Bryans was called and joined the crew prior to launch. On reaching the ship the doctor and Ruth went on board and, after a short time, it was decided to land the patient in Donaghadee to be transferred to hospital by ambulance.

October 17. Fishing vessel reported sinking off the Mull of Galloway and Donaghadee lifeboat was thought to be nearest in time from casualty. A Naval patrol arrived on scene at the same time as us and launched their Gemini rubber boat into a very turbulent sea where it was immediately swamped. The sailors did a great job keeping their engine running. The casualty was very low in the water, so it was most important that we got our salvage pump aboard the trawler, which was done very quickly by the Navy boys. They also transferred to us a young boy who was in shock and very cold to be attended to by Dr Bryans.

We had to tow the trawler very slowly at first as she was so low, but gradually we were able to increase our speed as our pump lowered the water level. This was one service where a vessel and three lives were definitely saved by the Navy and us.

December 4. Originally launched at midnight to search for a missing cabin cruiser, then asked to stand by and accompany Bangor lifeboat towing the cruiser to Bangor.

December 31. On exercise with Portpatrick lifeboat when we were diverted to the aid of yacht *Summer Madness* with a sick man aboard. When we arrived at the casualty the sea was very rough with swells about 10 feet, and great care had to be taken to transfer the patient as he had appeared to have had a stroke. We also brought the man's wife into the lifeboat, leaving one man to take the yacht on to Carrickfergus marina. We then proceeded to Portpatrick harbour where an ambulance was waiting to take the patient to Stranraer Hospital.

Later on that evening while we were on passage home we received another call from the Coastguard to *Summer Madness* which had engine trouble, so we diverted again and towed the yacht to Carrickfergus.

City of Belfast in a helicopter training day

January 28. A small tug making for Donaghadee harbour was having engine trouble and requested the lifeboat to stand by him if his engine was to stop and he was to be blown on to the rocks. The Honorary Secretary decided it would be prudent to have the lifeboat escort the tug into harbour, and this was done without incident.

April 9. A broken call was picked up by Belfast Coastguard saying three persons were stranded on the rocks at Maidens Rock lighthouse off Larne. The men had no radio or flares to attract attention but had broken in to the lighthouse buildings to use the radio there. We put our small rubber boat into the water and collected the three men and their boat from the rocks and landed them safely in Larne.

April 26. Responded to request for immediate launch that three persons were reported in the water off the coast of Ballywalter, but before reaching the scene a small rowing boat picked up the casualties. We continued on and recovered a Mirror dinghy, righted it and towed it to Ballywalter.

May 15. Belfast Coastguard launched the lifeboat in response to a call for assistance from a large fishing vessel *Ocean Trust* which had broken down in mid channel in a position the skipper said was twenty miles north of Donaghadee. When we worked out the position on the chart, the casualty was thirty six miles north of us and was really in Campbell-

1989

town lifeboat area, but since we were underway to the casualty we were told to proceed. This was another very large vessel and we had a long and uneventful tow to Larne Harbour.

May 5. A large Panamanian ship anchored off Carrickfergus requested the immediate services of a doctor to treat an engineer who had been burned by a blowback from the ship's boiler. Belfast Coastguard called on the lifeboat to launch which we did with the usual medical team of Dr Richard Bryans and Ruth Lennon aboard. After boarding the ship the doctor found the man was able to walk and a stretcher was not required, so we proceeded to Carrickfergus and transferred the patient to the waiting ambulance.

June 26. A mayday call was heard at 3 pm. The call was very brief: "Sinking south of Donaghadee," was all that was heard. *City of Belfast* was launched but had no defined search area so a helicopter was called to search a wider area. The south-westerly wind was strong with heavy rain squalls and the sea, covered with white tops, made it very difficult to see from the deck of the lifeboat. As the search continued and nothing was sighted, it began to seem like a hoax call, then information came through that a Galway Hooker – a type of sailing boat from the West of Ireland – and owned and sailed by Con McCann and his girlfriend was missing on passage from Portaferry to Bangor so the search continued until darkness, when we returned to station to refuel.

Next morning we left harbour at 5 am. The wind had dropped and it was a fine morning with good visibility, and after midday we started to pick up pieces of debris from the casualty. In the afternoon we had a crew change and shortly after, the Sea King helicopter sighted a girl's body in the water, recovered it, then lowered it onto the lifeboat to be landed in Portavogie. After this we continued the search for Con McCann until it was called off at 8 pm. Mr McCann's body was never found.

July 7. The Honorary Secretary was notified that a very large factory fishing trawler *Marella* was having engine difficulties and was only able to make two knots but was in no immediate danger. It was decided to postpone the lifeboat launch for 1 hour to see if any other vessels would help or if the engine could be repaired. On discussion with the Coastguard and me, the Honorary Secretary decided to launch as the tide had now turned and the ship was being carried away from the station. It was agreed to tow the vessel to the nearest safe harbour which was Bangor. This was completed without incident.

July 21. A small speedboat from Donaghadee was reported overdue so

City of Belfast was launched and, using parachute flares to aid the search, we quickly came on the casualty who was not in any real danger, having simply run out of fuel. Towed to Donaghadee.

August 8. Launched to go to the aid of a 38 foot motor launch *Sandpiper* which was adrift with engine failure in worsening weather. There were three persons aboard all suffering very badly with seasickness. The casualty was sixteen miles from the station and as visibility was good there was no trouble locating them. We towed them to Carrickfergus where the launch's crew were very happy to disembark.

August 17. Launched following a report from a fishing vessel having sighted red flares and been given the position of the casualty, we found a cabin cruiser *Catalina* with one man aboard adrift with no engine power. The occupant informed us that he had been under tow with another boat who had cast him off in mid channel and proceeded to Ballywalter harbour for fuel. We heard later that his companion had returned, and was unable to find him, returning again to Ballywalter. *Catalina* and lone sailor were taken to Donaghadee.

September 17. Six members of the crew and myself were invited to a naming ceremony being held in Howth harbour to name the new reserve lifeboat for Ireland, *Hibernia*. After the celebrations we were to have an exercise with the Howth lifeboat and then proceed to Donaghadee with *Hibernia* as *City of Belfast* was due to go for a refit. On our way north we came upon a small fishing boat *Le Shark* adrift and with no one aboard. It was trailing a rope with a lifebelt attached. No one seemed to know anything about this vessel but eventually the Skerries lifeboat came on scene and recognised the casualty as belonging to Rush and took the vessel in tow.

September 21. Vessel reported to Coastguards by telephone to be firing red flares approximately sixteen miles south of Donaghadee. After an extensive search was made it appeared to be a hoax. The hoax caller was later apprehended by the police.

September 22. A message was received from the occupant of a dive boat that he had a diver missing. We searched quite a bit down tide of the dive boat but found nothing so we extended the area and eventually found the missing diver on the rocks quite a long distance from his boat. This man was very lucky to make it to the rocks after such a long swim in the strong tidal stream. We recovered the diver in our Y class inflatable and landed him and his friend in Donaghadee.

October 30. Towed in a small rubber dinghy with engine breakdown.

City of Belfast goes to the aid of a stranded motorboat

November 3. A message was received from large drilling rig *Seillean* that they had a man badly injured and needed a doctor. We launched with Dr Bryans on board and proceeded to the ship, then stood by while the doctor treated the patient and decided to call on a helicopter to airlift the patient to hospital, before we returned to station.

1990

January 13. This was a wild day with a north-westerly wind blowing at over 50 knots – we had a struggle that day looking after our boats in the harbour.

At 10.30 in the evening we got a call to launch to help in the search for a fisherman who had been swept overboard from a large Fleetwood trawler. The search area was sixteen miles north-east of Donaghadee and it was a very rough ride to get there. On scene were three trawlers, a large cargo ship, and Portpatrick lifeboat. It was almost impossible to see a person in the water such was the height of the waves with the spray flying off the crests. We searched until long after dawn when it was decided to call off the search as it was felt that no one could survive such atrocious conditions.

January 17. Launched to escort small tanker *Breaksea* with engine trouble in mid channel to a safe anchorage in Belfast Lough without incident.

February 18. *Rocquaine,* a general cargo ship, reported to be having a bad leak, so *City of Belfast* was dispatched to meet the ship off Ballywalter. As it was a calm evening we were able to tie alongside the vessel to transfer our pump. Once this was done we continued to stand by until we reached the safety of Belfast harbour.

April 18. Launched in adverse weather conditions to aid yacht *Smij* of Antrim. Escorted the vessel to safety.

July 15. Large fishing trawler *Beulah* was leaking badly and needing assistance about twenty two miles from the station. Put lifeboat pump aboard then escorted the vessel to harbour.

July 18. A collision reported by fishing vessel *Sunlit Waters* having been struck by another boat and was badly damaged and making water, so again our salvage pump was brought into action. Escorted casualty to harbour.

July 27. Belfast Coastguard received a call from yacht *Foujean* that they had fouled their propeller and were in mid channel unable to make headway. *City of Belfast* was launched to tow the yacht the thirteen miles to Donaghadee.

July 29. The Coastguard on watch at Orlock Head reported seeing a yacht listing badly on the rocks in Chapel Bay on the large Copeland Island so he requested an immediate lifeboat launch. When we arrived on scene we could see people on the rocks beside the yacht. On speaking to the yacht's crew we found that she had broken her mooring and had drifted ashore, unmanned, as it was a falling tide. It was decided to land the two crew in Donaghadee and leave the skipper to bring the boat home when the tide rose.

August 5. At 3 am a request for launch was made by Belfast Coastguard saying a small cabin cruiser with an adult and two boys aboard was overdue on a fishing trip from Drummore in Luce Bay, Wigtownshire. Portpatrick lifeboat launched at the same time and both boats proceeded round the Mull of Galloway into Luce Bay to start our search. We set up searchlights and parachute flares – this small boat had no lights, radio or flares so we would have to be very close to see them. When we started out the wind was about force 3 from the north-west but after dawn it slowly increased to force 6 blowing directly off the land; there were a lot of small white tops on the waves which would have made a small white boat very hard to see. As the day progressed the search area was enlarged and more lifeboats were called to help. Stanraer inshore boat was brought by road to search the coastline. Kirkcudbright and Ramsay lifeboats were also asked to help and two helicopters were also brought in. The search continued all day. This was a very large area with strong tides and I felt sure with the amount of help some of us were bound to come across them but as darkness approached we were beginning to have our doubts. By this time our area was over forty miles away from the station.

As we sadly made our way home we felt it was almost certain that the boat was sunk and the occupants lost. Next morning as it was getting light a Portavogie trawler on its way to the fishing grounds came across the cabin cruiser with the occupants still aboard, very cold, very wet and very glad to be rescued so the story had a happy ending.

August 15. Belfast Coastguard requested an immediate launch to a small sailing dinghy three miles south of Donaghadee with four persons aboard. The Coastguards had been watching this craft approaching an area of breaking seas which were being whipped up by a force 7 north-west wind. As we came alongside we could see how close they were to the rough patch and would certainly have been swamped in a matter of minutes. The father and three sons were landed in Donaghadee none the worse for their experience.

September 23. A report of a yacht on the rocks at Copelands Marina and a man in the water. We were on scene in a few minutes to see the yachtsman was on the rocks trying to hold his boat off. We quickly put one of our crewmen on board the casualty to recover the man then pulled the boat off the rocks and towed to the harbour. The cause of the mishap was engine failure at the crucial moment of entering the narrow channel to the Marina.

October 8. Coastguard observed a small boat in some difficulty and was in radio contact with them saying that they had an intermittent fault with their engine. They kept in contact but eventually as the weather was worsening it was decided to send the lifeboat to assist them. On reaching the casualty we saw that this was a very frail craft so we felt it would be better to escort them while the engine was still going. Then the engine stopped and we were forced to make up a tow line which was difficult, as all our tow ropes were too thick to go round the little toy cleat which was only fastened to the deck with tiny screws. We had a small line on our rubber boat not much heavier than cord so we made this fast to the casualty and hoped for the best. We slowly made our way through the rough seas to Bangor Marina.

October 12. A request from Portpatrick lifeboat for assistance in towing a large steel trawler *Prevail* off the Mull of Galloway. The vessel was leaking badly and needed extra pumps. When we were a couple of miles from Portpatrick it was decided to land the ship's crew there as their partner boat was to continue the tow to Girvan. We were then released and returned to station.

November 10. Word came to the station that fishing vessel *Neiried* was on the rocks at Donaghadee Marina entrance 500 yards from the harbour. We were able to get alongside and put one of our crew onboard with a towrope and towed her to Donaghadee harbour where we put our pump aboard to control the flow of water until a local boat took her to the Marina to be lifted by the crane.

November 10. Second call today. We were advised by the Coastguard that *HMS Helford* had a man on board with a suspected heart attack. We were delayed a short time trying to contact a doctor, but had to leave without one. The ship was six miles east of Donaghadee. We transferred the patient to the lifeboat and Dr Bryans advised by radio what action to take and arranged to meet us in Bangor Marina where he had contacted the cardiac ambulance. The doctor and paramedics spent a fairly long time treating the patient in the lifeboat before transfer to hospital.

November 23. We were called out to search in very rough conditions, gale force 8, for a light aircraft. Portpatrick was also out searching, but the position given to us was later changed to being inland so our search was called off.

December 28. A report from Belfast-Stranraer ferry *Galloway Princess* saying they had lost a man overboard in very rough conditions. We launched at 11 pm into the gale and we felt we had little hope of success as the ferry was fifteen miles north of us. After searching for three hours Belfast Coastguard called off the search as it was long past the maximum exposure time for those conditions. The following day the ferry reported a mistake in their head count.

February 27. Launched to aid a small fishing boat adrift at the mouth of Belfast Lough with broken down gearbox, towed to Bangor without incident.

1991

March 11. Motor cruiser *Nimrod* was reported on the rocks in Whitehead Bay in thick fog with three people on board. The lifeboat pulled it off the rocks and inspected it for damage, where it was found that the steering gear was broken. Towed to Bangor.

April 6. Yacht *Sea Spell* with four men aboard was trying to enter Strangford Lough, but was advised not to attempt it in the south east gale force

Graham McConnell,
Coxswain 1991-1995

conditions. Portaferry inshore lifeboat was unable to cross the entrance bar, so we escorted the yacht to Donaghadee.

April 13. Asked to launch by Liverpool Coastguard to help large fishing vessel *Lady Ann* with three crew with total engine failure and unsure of his position but he believed he was twelve miles south east of Donaghadee.

When we arrived at this position we could see no sign of any vessel; we had been trying to make radio contact without success, so in the hope that they could hear us we asked them to fire a flare. This was sighted twelve miles further east in Luce Bay. We proceeded there and found the vessel which we towed to Portpatrick.

May 8. Trawler *Accord* making water rapidly and needing a pump quickly so a helicopter was scrambled with a pump. The Coastguard decided to send the lifeboat as back up. The vessel was sixteen miles south of Donaghadee, there was no wind and the sea was flat calm so we reached the casualty in less than an hour to discover the ship was still making water and the pump the helicopter left wouldn't start, so we tied alongside, put our pump on board with two men and a little later we managed to get the other pump started. We then escorted *Accord* to Portavogie.

This was to be my last service in charge of *City of Belfast* as I retired on my birthday, which is May 13th. Next morning I had a very pleasant surprise; in the post was a letter telling me I had been honoured by the Queen and was to be awarded the British Empire Medal.

Graham McConnell took over as the new coxswain and David Martin was 2nd coxswain.

August 14. Asked by Coastguard to escort fishing vessel *Quiet Man* as she was leaking but her own pumps were coping with the water. Escorted to Portavogie without incident.

September 1. *City of Belfast* was on exercise when asked to assist a small speed boat with engine breakdown. Towed to Groomsport.

September 3. Launched at Coastguard's request to a vessel thought to have lost its rudder in thick fog. Intercepted the vessel which was still underway to discover that it was the radar that was lost; as the fog had cleared he was able to continue to Belfast.

February 15. Yacht *Imp* reported to be dismasted, with no engine and six people on board. The position given was one mile south of Copeland Island. Launched and towed the casualty to Bangor Marina.

1992

March 17. *MV Belgrave* reported aground on Copeland island but not requesting assistance and not responding to radio calls. It was just after high water so the lifeboat was sent to investigate. The skipper confirmed the ship was hard aground and unable to refloat under her own power. The coxswain offered a tow which was accepted without enthusiasm by the skipper but he was amazed when the *City of Belfast* pulled his ship off on a falling tide. Escorted a short time until the skipper was happy to proceed on his way.

April 27. Launched to check out a motor cruiser adrift four miles northeast of the station. Located and found no one aboard. Towed to Donaghadee and we later found out it had broken away from a mooring in Groomsport.

May 22. Set out in thick fog and calm sea to search for yacht *Camille*, which was unable to give position other than they had hit rocks. Visibility was down to a few yards but the direction finder was used to get near the casualty. The yacht was so close inshore the Y class inflatable had to be used to run a rope to them. Towed to Donaghadee.

May 25. Belfast Coastguard requested the lifeboat to meet fishing vessel *Moussaillon* six miles south of the station. One of their crew was running a high temperature and severe stomach pains and in need of medical help. On reaching the casualty Dr Bryans boarded the vessel and after his examination authorised the transfer to the lifeboat and to the waiting ambulance for the onward trip to hospital.

June 14. *City of Belfast* was on exercise with 2nd coxswain David Martin in charge when a yacht reported to him that a group of windsurfers seemed to be in trouble. On approaching the group all were very tired and distressed. Landed them in Donaghadee.

June 26. Irish Lights Tender *Granuaile* struck rocks at Maidens Lighthouse and was in sinking condition. Helicopters landed pumps on the vessel and the lifeboat added theirs but it was to no avail as the water was still rising. The master, Captain Hook, decided that to save his ship he would have to drive her ashore on the nearest sandy beach which was Brown's Bay, Islandmagee, which he did successfully. There were forty one persons on *Granuaile*. One fireman was unconscious and two others were landed in Larne. Stood by all night in case of further emergencies, returning to station at midday.

August 1. Launched to go to the aid of yacht *Vagrant* fourteen miles south of Donaghadee, which had steering problems in very adverse conditions. On reaching the casualty the coxswain decided to tow the yacht to Portavogie as the yachtsmen were very seasick and this was the nearest safe harbour.

September 27. Asked to search for an open fishing boat *White Heather* lost in the fog with six persons on board. With *White Heather* transmitting on VHF radio the lifeboat was able to home in on her using the radio direction finder. On arrival alongside they found the casualty had fouled its propeller by becoming entangled in some lobster pots.

Philip McNamara, a trained diver on the crew, freed the rope from the shaft and the vessel was able to follow the lifeboat to Carrickfergus.

September 28. The same fog banks were still causing trouble; a small boat with 2 hp outboard motor was overdue with two occupants and no radio. This was a difficult service because it was very hard to distinguish the radar echo of such a small craft and the outlying rocks. Eventually they were found anchored fairly close inshore in a distressed state, one of the men having heart problems. Towed to Donaghadee.

November 23. A request from Belfast Coastguard for a launch to large fishing vessel *Fionela*. Position given was twenty four miles south-east of the station. The wind was gale force from the south so it was a very bumpy ride to the casualty which, incidentally, was much farther south

A tight squeeze!

than was first intimated. When the lifeboat arrived on scene there were twenty foot swells making it impossible to get alongside unless in an absolute emergency. A helicopter came on scene and lowered pumps onto the stricken vessel's deck, then started the slow escort duty to Bangor harbour. Coxswain and crew reported the heroic work carried out by the helicopter winchman who, on being lowered to the vessel's deck, was totally submerged several times in the twenty foot waves before managing to land on deck.

1993

January 28. At 5.30 pm reports came in of a crashed aircraft in Belfast Lough. *City of Belfast* carried out an extensive search of the area until midnight but nothing was found.

January 29. 7 am. Continued service to search for the crashed light aircraft. Searched Belfast Lough extensively but only wreckage was found. Recalled at 1.15 pm but launched again at 3 pm to assist in the location and recovery of a body. Bangor lifeboat landed the pilot's body in Bangor harbour.

April 4. Alerted by Coastguard that a jet ski was in trouble in Ballyhalbert Bay. On arrival the lifeboat found two persons in the water holding on to an inflated inner tube which had the sunken jet ski suspended below. One of the casualties was a girl who was suffering from an asthma attack and slight hypothermia. The lifeboat crew recovered the jet ski and arranged for an ambulance to meet them at Donaghadee. The doctor was not available, but paramedic Ruth Lennon came to the station with an asthma inhaler and assisted until the ambulance arrived. Both survivors were wearing wetsuits but the girl's condition suggested that she might not have survived a much longer period of immersion.

April 8. Requested to launch to yacht *Irish Mist* to assist crew to restrain a psychiatric patient who had become unruly. In the yacht's area the wind was force 7 with twelve foot swells and Coxswain McConnell felt that with such motion between the boats, it was too dangerous to attempt a transfer for fear the patient would jump overboard. The lifeboat stood by in close quarters to Donaghadee and the waiting ambulance.

April 20. Message received from yacht *Voltaire*, "In very rough conditions and making water. Need help". Launched to go to position given fourteen miles north of station. The weather conditions were very rough with a wind force of gale 8, and a five metre swell. On arriving on scene the yacht was rolling wildly and the three men on board were very seasick. The coxswain felt it would be better to put a lifeboatman aboard to connect the tow line as the yacht's crew were too ill to be of much help. After towing *Voltaire* for an hour and a half the life boat received another message from Belfast Coastguard stating that a fisherman had fallen overboard from his vessel twenty miles to the south. The lifeboat had to continue to tow the yacht for another forty minutes until the sea state allowed Bangor inshore lifeboat to take over the tow.

As a long search was anticipated and lifeboat was passing station some crew changes were made on the way to the second casualty. The sea conditions in the search area were atrocious with 10 metre swells.

The vessel *Berachah,* from which the man had fallen, was leading the search along with quite a number of trawlers. The search continued for five hours until midnight but nothing was found.

May 3. Informed by the Coastguard of a person missing since the previous day. His car was found convenient to the beach. The lifeboat requested to have a short search, but nothing was found. A body was washed up 10 miles farther north one week later.

June 6. Cabin cruiser *Shark Bait* with broken down engine. Towed to Copelands Marina to be lifted out.

July 12. A report of small open boat adrift behind the Copeland Island with five persons aboard. Found and towed to Donaghadee without incident.

July 19. Coastguard alerted the coxswain of a catamaran capsized in Ballyhalbert Bay with one man in the water and requested an immediate launch. On reaching the scene the yacht was in fairly shallow water, completely upside down with its mast hitting bottom. The occupant was holding on to the boat's hull so the coxswain decided to launch the Y class inflatable to recover the yachtsman and right the catamaran. After this was done the boat and owner were taken to the beach.

August 7. At nearly midnight a yacht was reported to be on the rocks at Briggs Reef, Groomsport with six people on board. *City of Belfast* was launched and it was found that the yacht had refloated and was clear of the rocks but was making so little headway and, being unsure of their position, they asked to be towed to Bangor Marina.

September 20. Launched on information from the Coastguard regarding a small motor boat with engine failure with three people requiring assistance; located and towed to Donaghadee.

September 22. Yacht *Low Profile* reported losing its rudder and requiring immediate help. Wind at the time was northerly, force 6-7 with three metre swells. The yacht was crewed by an adult and two children. The man asked the coxswain to take the children into the lifeboat as they were seasick and very frightened. Coxswain was unhappy to go alongside in the rough conditions for risk of damage to the yacht and suggested a tow to Donaghadee. The children's father pleaded to have them transferred, regardless of damage. Coxswain McConnell then manoeuvred the lifeboat close enough to get a crewman aboard the yacht to help transfer the children to the lifeboat. This was carried out successfully without any damage due to excellent boat handling by the coxswain.

October 8. 2nd coxswain David Martin received a phone call from Mew Island lighthouse to say a small boy had been injured in a fall on Old Lighthouse Island. The lifeboat launched at 1.45 pm into a strong breeze from the east whipping up steep seas in the strong tide races round the islands. I happened to be on the pier when the maroons were fired and David asked me to make up the crew numbers as they were a man short.

On arrival at the island we discovered the boy was the son of the present coxswain, Philip McNamara. We lay in the shelter of the island and the family was ferried out to us in the birdwatcher's boat. The boy was bleeding from his nose and mouth. He was taken to hospital where we learned he had a broken jaw.

October 14. Belfast Coastguard requested an immediate launch to go to assist fishing vessel *Achieve* which had snagged an underwater cable with its fishing gear and was listing badly. I was again asked to make up crew numbers as the coxswain and mechanic were away at this time. When we arrived on scene we were able to help cut the fishing gear away and then towed *Achieve* to Donaghadee without further incident.

November 26. Launched in response to a mayday call from cabin cruiser *Heather Anne* saying that they were on the rocks at the west side of Copeland Island. The lifeboat was quickly on scene as the casualty was only two miles from the station only to find the cruiser high and dry; she had been holed. The lifeboat sent their Y class inflatable to ferry the elderly gentleman over and proceeded to Donaghadee.

December 26. Reports of a small fishing boat apparently broken down in a dangerous position near Maidens Lighthouse off Larne. The lifeboat found the casualty anchored in a strong tidal stream and unable to lift the anchor so the rope had to be cut. It was then towed to Larne. The coxswain felt the two men had been very lucky to have their anchor hold when they were only 150 yards from the rocks.

1994

March 15. Requested to launch to assist a large cruiser with engine failure twenty five miles north of the station which was towed to Bangor Marina. This was a difficult tow in the lumpy conditions, with the tow rope breaking twice en route.

May 28. Trainee 2nd coxswain Philip McNamara was in charge of the relief lifeboat and was returning to station after an exercise and display in Bangor when he noticed a Ministry of Defence fast motor launch firing a red smoke signal. On finding it to have engine trouble, it was towed to Bangor with two persons landed.

June 25. A vessel was reported lost in the fog. The casualty said he was not in immediate danger and near a large landmass but he had no idea where he was. Launched just after midnight, the lifeboat found the cruiser by direction finder and escorted it to Carrickfergus. On passage to station at 2.30 am when they were informed of another yacht, *Intravenous,* lost in the fog and requesting assistance to find Bangor Marina. She was found and escorted to Bangor, leaving for station at 4.30 am.

July 17. Motor boat *Tango 1* suffered engine failure and was towed to Donaghadee.

July 24. Yacht *Coranto* suffered engine failure. Towed to Donaghadee.

July 28. Motor boat *Emily 2* experienced engine failure. Towed to Donaghadee.

August 14. Fishing vessel *Nimbus* with engine failure. Towed to Bangor.

September 10. Cabin cruiser *Alexandra* suffered engine failure. Towed to Donaghadee.

This spate of tow jobs were carried out in calm weather and without incident.

1995

January 6. Coastguards observed a large Russian merchant vessel drifting without power and they were not able to contact it by radio. The lifeboat was asked by the Coastguard to launch to investigate. The vessel got underway as soon as the lifeboat approached. Returned to station.

January 8. Request for immediate launch to search for a man overboard from large merchant vessel *Northgate*. This man had not been missed for five hours so the search area was extremely large. Lifeboats from Newcastle, Port St. Mary and Clogher Head were also in the search area. Donaghadee lifeboat launched at 6.10 pm, and at one stage the search pattern took the lifeboat fifty miles south of the station. The searchers were hampered by the darkness and the rough conditions, and the search was abandoned after eight hours with sadly nothing found.

April 6. Launched on a medical emergency to channel ferry *Stena Antrim* with Dr Richard Bryans and paramedic Ruth McNamara aboard. The ferry was twenty miles away from the station so a helicopter was also scrambled. On arrival on scene, the casualty was being airlifted to hospital. Returned to station.

April 30. Responded to a phone call from a bird-watching party on Old Lighthouse Island saying that a man had fallen on the rocks and was injured. Waited for Dr Bryans and Ruth McNamara (now married) then launched. At the island the coxswain used the Y class inflatable to get the medics ashore. On examination the doctor found the man's injuries were considerably worse than first thought. The casualty was, however, able to walk with assistance as it was thought to be too dangerous for a stretcher on the steep cliff path. Landed in Donaghadee to a waiting ambulance. The birdwatcher had sustained a dislocated shoulder, broken ribs and numerous abrasions.

David Martin
Coxswain 1995-1999

June 4. Request at 3.30 am to tow in a fishing vessel with engine trouble. Found *Fiddler's Green* fifteen miles south of station and towed it to Portavogie.

June 12. Reports of a vessel unsure of his position. Using the direction finder, the vessel was tracked to Luce Bay, Scotland, totally off course from Isle of Man to Newcastle. Towed to Donaghadee. The coxswain's opinion was that conditions were most unsuitable for such a small boat with four people onboard to try to cross from the Isle of Man to Ireland.

June 26. Motor boat *Red Rhum* reported with engine trouble and anchored in a dangerous position near rocks six miles south of station. The vessel was found and towed to Donaghadee.

August 20. Launched in response to mayday distress call from fishing boat *Kindly Light* twelve miles south of the station. On arrival on scene the lifeboat found a local trawler had *Kindly Light* on tow. Escorted them safely to Portavogie.

Coxswain Graham McConnell retired and his position was taken over by David Martin. His position of 2nd coxswain was taken over by Philip McNamara.

October 29. Belfast Coastguard requested an immediate launch in response to a report of a man overboard from merchant vessel *Galway Bank* in Belfast Lough. Searched along with Bangor and Larne lifeboats and two helicopters. The search was terminated after ten hours with nothing found.

1996

April 27. Report of a woman with a known medical complaint who had forgotten her medication and in need of emergency evacuation from one of the Copeland Islands. Dr Bryans suggested that the lifeboat should proceed and he would meet the casualty at the harbour. This was carried out without incident.

May 6. Launched to help small fishing boat *Aileen* drifting near rocks with engine trouble and their engine room full of smoke, thought to be from electrical fault. Towed to Bangor harbour.

May 31. Coastguard requested a launch to recover a drifting speedboat which could become a hazard to navigation. Towed to Donaghadee.

June 1. Informed by the Coastguard that a large steel fishing vessel *Rosamunda* was leaking badly and was very unstable and required the lifeboat to stand by as a precaution. The vessel was found twelve miles away and escorted to Bangor harbour where she was pumped out by the Fire Brigade.

July 3. Asked to search for a small boat which had reported engine failure by mobile phone to Belfast Coastguard. Located the small open boat with two persons on board four miles south. Towed to Donaghadee.

July 13. Request for help from yacht *Ceteway* which was becalmed and had propeller trouble. Towed to Bangor Marina.

August 3. Helicopter and *City of Belfast* were on a flag day exercise and display when they were diverted to the aid of a yacht club rescue boat. Other vessels helped and after checking everyone was safe, the lifeboat returned to station.

August 31. *Lady Nicole,* a small fishing boat, was drifting and in danger of going onto rocks. She could be seen from the station, and was quickly taken in tow back to harbour.

October 16. Launched in response to a red flare fired from small fishing vessel *Sea Mist* seen from the station. Vessel had lost all battery power so was towed to Donaghadee.

December 7. Called out to large motor cruiser *Alvista* which, in the poor visibility, was unsure of its position. Found the vessel just in time as she was heading between the Copeland Islands and would surely have grounded. Escorted to Donaghadee but both engines failed at the critical moment of entering the harbour. The lifeboat quickly got a rope aboard and towed her through the entrance. They also had a fire in their engine room caused by a jammed starter motor.

1997

March 29. Requested to launch to a small fishing boat adrift in Donaghadee Sound. Located and towed to harbour.

April 5. Launched on report of a missing diver. Commenced box search with Portpatrick lifeboat and helicopter and, after searching for five hours, the diver was spotted by the helicopter in an area not previously covered by the lifeboats, but was directly ahead of the *City of Belfast* search pattern 1 mile ahead.

May 18. Yacht *Penboch Too* was unsure of its position and had fouled the propeller on a string of lobster pots. Located in Belfast Lough and towed to Bangor.

June 8. Belfast Coastguard requested the help of the lifeboat for a small boat with three persons on board who were unsure of their position and had fuel trouble on passage from the Isle of Man. Located vessel which had been taken in tow by a merchant ship. Transferred the tow and continued to Donaghadee.

July 20. Reports came in of two persons stranded on an offshore rock which was soon to be covered by the incoming tide. The lifeboat launched and proceeded to the scene to find that one of the young men had managed to swim ashore. The other lad could not swim and had spent two hours on the rock, luckily in good weather. Transferred to lifeboat and brought to Donaghadee. The boys had bought an inflatable boat some hours earlier and, after paddling to the rock, they decided to lift the boat out and sit on it. BANG! No boat left, just a bit of plastic.

July 22. Towed in a broken down cabin cruiser near Donaghadee.

July 31. Launched to assist a speedboat which was out of fuel and drifting offshore. Towed in.

August 7. Coastguard requested a launch to search for two missing divers but recalled the lifeboat just after leaving the harbour as the divers were picked up by a passing fishing boat. These divers were very lucky to have been located as their dive boat was completely in the wrong area

Front row (l-r): Ross Bennett, Steven McComiskey, Philip McNamara, John Ashwood, John Allen. Back row (l-r): Alan McCulla, George Thompson, David McCormack, Richard McGimpsey

over a mile away and on the wrong side of the island.

August 13. Yacht *Foam.* Unsure of his position in the fog and with a faulty engine. Located and towed to Donaghadee.

August 24. *City of Belfast* was on exercise when the Coastguard diverted them to yacht *Castaway* on the Briggs rocks. No damage was sustained and it was towed off and taken to Bangor Marina.

August 31. Advised of an elderly man on the main Copeland Island unable to move and in need of medivac – a medical evacuation. The lifeboat awaited the arrival of Dr Bryans then launched. When on the scene some of the crew were landed to carry the casualty down to the lifeboat then on to Donaghadee to be taken away by ambulance.

August 31. At 8 pm the same evening the Coastguard reported a yacht *Twister* aground on South Briggs Reef. As the tide was low, it was too shallow for the lifeboat to get close to the casualty so they had to use the Y class inflatable to pass the towrope and examine the yacht for damage. After successfully towing the yacht off the reef she was taken to Bangor Marina. On the way the Coastguard was advised that one of the yacht's crew was suffering very badly from cold and needed medical attention.

September 6. Catamaran *Freyia* with one man on board was reported to be breaking up fifteen miles south of the station. It was located and towed slowly to Portavogie. Several weeks later the owner of *Freyia*, a member of the army, visited the crew to pass on his thanks.

October 25. The Coastguard requested a search for an overdue tug. The vessel was located at anchor with engine failure. Towed to Donaghadee.

November 10. Large fishing vessel *Deborah* reported a crewman missing in an approximate position six miles north west of base. Launched at 8 pm and searched a wide area with Bangor lifeboat and several trawlers. The search was called off at midnight after a body was sighted by one of the trawlers and picked up by Bangor lifeboat.

November 24. Received a report of a large merchant vessel *Wave* of Cyprus having problems with the high winds, breaking mooring ropes to Clochan jetty near Whitehead. *City of Belfast* launched at 12 midnight and proceeded to the scene. The ship was in danger of being blown ashore so the lifeboat was asked to stand by until tugs arrived to push her back alongside the jetty. Stood by until 4 am, then returned to station.

1998

January 2. Requested to go to the help of large fishing vessel *North Sea Coast* with steering and engine problems 10 miles south of the station. When the lifeboat made contact, communications were very difficult with the Spanish crew. The vessel was able to maintain a speed of five knots so it was decided, due to her size, to escort her to Belfast.

January 15. The lifeboat was asked to launch to take over from Newcastle lifeboat which was standing by a small merchant vessel *Al Masooma* in a position twenty two miles south of Donaghadee. On relieving the Newcastle boat they found the coaster was making slow headway and escorted until the Newcastle men returned to escort the casualty into Dundrum Bay. Returned to station.

February 8. A report from Belfast Coastguard came through that a man had sustained injuries on the Belfast to Liverpool ferry, *Lagan Viking* ,and needed a medivac. On trying to stay alongside in the heavy swell the lifeboat suffered slight damage to the guardrails, but eventually the doctor was able to board the vessel. Great difficulty was experienced getting the stretcher back aboard the lifeboat, followed by the man's baby in a carry cot and lastly the casualty's wife. During these transfers, lifeboatman Michael Fields slipped on the wet deck and suffered a badly broken leg. Returned to Donaghadee and sent the casualties to hospital by ambulance.

Philip McNamara
Coxswain 1999-present

May 17. Request from a member of a bird-watching group direct to the coxswain for medical assistance for a man on Old Lighthouse Island who had severe abdominal pains. Dr Bryans was summoned and the lifeboat launched. On arrival at the island, the doctor was ferried ashore by Y class inflatable and, after examination, decided that the casualty was not serious and further assistance was not required.

June 19. Fishing vessel *Investor,* returning from the fishing grounds, had an engine failure twenty miles south of the station. Located and towed to Portavogie without incident.

June 28. Tobermory lifeboat was just leaving Donaghadee on her delivery trip when Belfast Coastguard announced that a yacht, *Sun Trapper,* was aground on Horse Point on Copeland Island. Tobermory lifeboat stood by the casualty for a few minutes until *City of Belfast* came on scene. The yacht was in shallow water so the towrope had to be taken in by Y class inflatable. When the casualty was refloated, it was towed to Donaghadee.

July 2. *Sun Trapper* again in trouble, this time having a lobster pot foul her propeller just after being launched at Copelands Marina after having a survey because of the previous incident. Saw her safely into harbour.

July 3. Launched to help barge *Dolphin* with gearbox trouble. Located and towed to Donaghadee.

July 28. Belfast Coastguard informed the lifeboat that two children had been cut off by the incoming tide on outlying rocks at Millisle. When on scene the Y class inflatable was used to convey the children safely to the beach.

July 30. The Coastguard requested an immediate launch in very rough conditions to go to the aid of yacht *Serendipity* which had been dismasted sixteen miles south of station. Found the casualty and towed slowly to Donaghadee, where the crew were landed very cold, tired and a bit shocked but not needing medical attention.

August 2. A large power boat was adrift near the station with engine trouble. Towed into harbour.

1999

January 5. Vessel reported to be firing red flares. Launched to go to a position six miles south east of the station where the lifeboat found fishing vessel *Christelle* with no engine power and just in the process of being towed by another trawler. Stood by until safely berthed in Ballywalter.

April 2. Called out to help yacht *Susie Ann* which had run out of fuel and could not sail in the calm conditions. Located and towed to Donaghadee.

This was David Martin's last service as coxswain before retiring, having served twenty one years as a crewman and officer. Philip McNamara was promoted to coxswain.

May 21. Launched to go to aid large training yacht *Lord Rank* owned by the Ocean Youth Club which was having engine trouble, causing problems in manoeuvring. The lifeboat found the yacht sailing in open water but they requested to be towed into Bangor Marina. This was completed without incident.

May 31. Belfast Coastguard requested a launch to investigate an upturned hull sighted by a fishing vessel. Located and identified it as *Nomad* and towed it into Donaghadee. Later Coastguards reported that *Nomad* had been abandoned two days earlier. No lives lost or persons missing.

June 19. Tug *Warrior* reported to have hit an underwater object and was leaking badly, with six men aboard. An immediate launch was called. On escorting the casualty into Bangor Harbour the tug men had to negotiate a fee for pumping out the water with the local fire brigade. While this was in progress the lifeboat crew pumped the water out.

June 22. Another call to a leaking vessel, a small fishing boat *Lisa Jane,* which had taken a lot of water in her engine room. When the lifeboat got on scene the casualty was under tow by another fishing boat. Escorted them into Portavogie and then pumped out the water.

June 28. A Manx yacht *Celosia* had grounded on the rocks at the entrance to Copelands marina. As the weather was so calm and the yacht was sitting upright on her twin keels, the coxswain did not want to risk damage by towing her off. The skipper was happy to wait for the next high tide, and the yacht refloated successfully and entered the marina without help.

July 8. A very dense fog on this day. A request to launch from the Coastguards to search for a yacht *Capilanyo* which was unsure of its position. Located the yacht quite near the harbour and guided in.

July 8. At 11 pm that night people on shore heard shouts for help and reported to the Coastguards. The lifeboat was launched and they located small power boat *Dove* out of fuel. Towed in.

July 21. A large power boat *Andragon* was reported to have hit an underwater object and had damaged or lost both propellers. The lifeboat found her adrift outside Portavogie harbour and towed her safely inside.

August 4. Belfast Coastguard requested a launch to search for two persons overdue in a small rowing boat. The small boat was located by another boat and handed the tow over to the lifeboat which landed them in Donaghadee.

September 7. This is a service that I know of first hand. I had just landed on Mew Island with my son-in-law Shane McNamara and a friend when I suffered very severe chest pains. Luckily John Magowan had a GTN spray and this seemed to help the pain. In the meantime Shane had radioed ashore, the lifeboat was on the way and in a short time they had me aboard and on oxygen. This was my first time on board *City of Belfast* as a customer. Waiting for me on the harbour were the cardiac team and paramedics and I spent the next week in the Cardiac Unit in Ulster Hospital. This experience brought home to me the importance of the training sessions.

2000

April 30. A mayday was put out by a 30 foot motor cruiser saying both engines had failed and the boat was drifting in the very strong tide 1 mile north-east of Donaghadee. The owner was concerned that the wind and tide would put him on the rocks nearby. The lifeboat was launched and met *Cat of Nine Tails* which, by this time, was making slow progress on one engine which was working erratically. The casualty had been making for Carrickfergus but the lifeboat coxswain Philip McNamara suggested they return to Donaghadee for repairs. This vessel had been in a very dangerous area before being escorted to harbour.

June 1. Launched because of a mayday message from a large power boat, *Magnum.* Portpatrick was also called as this vessel was twenty miles away from Donaghadee. Because of the distance for the two boats to travel, a helicopter was also alerted and a merchant ship stood by the liferaft. The helicopter was on scene quickly and winched the three survivors aboard. The lifeboats arrived and searched the area to confirm the vessel had sunk. Some debris and one semi-inflated lifejacket were picked up. The lifeboats then retuned to station.

June 4. Liverpool Coastguard received a radio message from a catamaran reporting that they were taking water and were unsure of their position (somewhere between Isle of Man and the Irish coast when radio contact was lost). A major search was organised with four lifeboats – Peel, Port Erin, Portaferry and Donaghadee. Eventually contact was made close to the Irish coast and well away from the search area. Located by helicopter. Donaghadee lifeboat stood by while casualty was towed in by Portaferry. Sea conditions were very rough with the wind north-east force 7.

June 12. Large motor cruiser *Clanricarde* was putting out mayday distress signals and the lifeboat found the cruiser with a very vigorous fire in her engine room. When the engine was stopped the fire was quickly brought under control before the casualty was towed to harbour. The fire was caused by a soundproofing panel falling onto the hot turbo charger, and also a severed oil pipe.

June 27. Belfast Coastguard reported a small boat adrift with engine failure. Located and towed to Donaghadee. The rescue was without incident or a word of thanks from the casualty.

June 28. A call to the same boat. This vessel was not seaworthy, at least mechanically, and Walker Simpson, the lifeboat mechanic, advised the owner not to take the boat to sea again without an overhaul.

July 9. A member of the public reported the capsizing of a small sailing dinghy near Ballywalter with two people in the water. On arriving on scene they found a small speedboat with one casualty aboard and one still in the water. The man in the water was very reluctant to leave his upturned boat but was brought into the lifeboat as he was so cold, having been immersed for over thirty minutes. Two lifeboatmen had to

(l-r): Philip McNamara, Willie Lennon, Walker Simpson, Robert Erskine, Graham McConnell and Jim Bunting

enter the water to assist. It was decided to let the speedboat tow the dinghy ashore as the coxswain felt it would be better to have the casualties examined by the doctor who was waiting at the station.

July 10. Belfast Coastguard advised the station Honorary Secretary at 2.30 am that yacht *Sprayoa* was making for Donaghadee but was running very low on fuel. There was a force 6-7 wind blowing from the north, whipping up a moderate sea making it too dangerous to attempt coming closer with an unreliable engine. *City of Belfast* launched and proceeded to the yacht's position which, by this time, was about four miles away. The lifeboat towed the yacht to outside the harbour where the skipper decided to start his engine to enter the harbour mouth. The engine failed to start so the tow continued through the confused swell. Crew members ashore took ropes and prevented the heavy vessel damaging moored boats in the harbour.

July 11. A report of a yachtsman onboard *Jezebel* being taken ill. The lifeboat launched with paramedic Ruth McNamara in the crew and proceeded to the position fifteen miles south of the station. On examination Ruth advised a medivac, so the patient was transferred to the lifeboat and landed in Portavogie to a waiting ambulance.

(l-r): Shane McNamara, John Ashwood, John Allen, George Hackworth, John Petrie, Philip McNamara, George Thompson (kneeling), Ian Couser, Steven McComiskey

2001

February 15. A mayday was heard by Belfast Coastguard at 2.17 am from *Audentia*. By 2.30 the engine room was half full and rising quickly. Two other fishing boats, *Investor* and *Ben Loyal,* were approaching. All four crewmen were taken aboard *Ben Loyal* unhurt. Donaghadee and Peel lifeboats were asked to continue, and just as Peel lifeboat came on scene the casualty rolled over and exposed a large gash on her starboard bow. Only debris was left floating on the surface which included a liferaft picked up by Donaghadee lifeboat.

April 17. At 11.47 pm Donaghadee lifeboat launched and proceeded at full speed to a position off the coast at Ardglass where there had been a collision between two large fishing boats, *Walpole* and *Azure Sea*. *Walpole* had lost all power and steering and was taking in water. The engine of *Azure Sea* was also stopped and she was drifting. On arrival Donaghadee lifeboat put a crewman and their salvage pump aboard *Walpole*. Portaferry lifeboat assisted in this procedure and the tow was commenced towards Ardglass harbour. While this was in progress Newcastle lifeboat towed *Azure Sea* into harbour and retuned to assist steering *Walpole* into harbour. This was completed without further incident.

April 26. A report was received from a Dutch motor vessel *Arrow* requesting the assistance of a doctor to attend to an eye injury of one of the crew. Dr Neill was contacted and the lifeboat made the short trip offshore to where the vessel was lying. The doctor was able to treat the patient on board and advised to seek further medical help at the next port of call.

August 13. The lifeboat responded to several 999 calls from members of the public. A person was seen to be adrift on a home-made raft off the coast of Ballyhalbert. While the lifeboat was on passage a local boat rescued the man and his raft. The lifeboat returned to base.

September 1. Coastguards advised the lifeboat that a 14 foot speedboat had broken down and was being blown offshore by the wind. On arrival at the scene the casualty was taken in tow back towards the shore at Millisle where a friend came out and took over the tow with the lifeboat standing by.

October 1. Reports of a woman walking into the sea fully dressed, and that she could not be restrained by those present. The crew was assembled, three of the officers and crew entered the water and dragged her out, under severe protest of the female. The doctor and ambulance men treated her at the scene. She had had a lot to drink and had been asked to leave a local bar shortly before the incident.

November 16. A passenger was reported missing when the Belfast-Stranraer ferry arrived in Stranraer. The Portpatrick and Donaghadee lifeboats were tasked to search the route as the man had been last seen when the vessel was leaving Belfast Lough and could have gone missing anywhere from there to Stranraer. The search was called off after 3.5 hours.

December 11. The *Warrior Maid* had just left Copelands Marina when she had an engine failure. The boat was drifting towards the rocks at the back of the harbour and her anchor was not holding, so the lifeboat was asked to help. A line was thrown to the vessel and it was towed safely into harbour.

After 17 years of service, *City of Belfast* stood down to be replaced by *Saxon,* having been launched 153 times and saved 35 lives.

Saxon

Saxon is welcomed to Donaghadee

January 2. RIB *Predator* left Portpatrick at 1 am en route to Donaghadee. The weather was fine when they left but later in the trip the sea became rough and their speed was reduced. Eventually they ran out of fuel and lost all power including lights and radio. One of the occupants had a mobile phone and used it to contact Belfast Coastguard. Now a small rubber boat with no lights is very hard to locate, but the man in the RIB was able to direct the lifeboat by phone. At 3.50 am it was spotted and taken in tow to Donaghadee.

February 17. A call was received from the Coastguard at 7 am that a tug towing another had engine trouble off the Scottish coast. Donaghadee lifeboat arrived on scene at 8.45 am and stood by as the engine had been restarted. In the meantime Portpatrick lifeboat took aboard a man who was suffering from hypothermia. A short time after this, the tug's engine failed again and Donaghadee had to take both tugs in tow to keep them from being blown ashore. At 1 pm another tug arrived on scene and took

2003

The naming ceremony of the *Saxon*

over the tow. The lifeboats were released and returned to their bases.

February 18. Belfast Coastguard reported a fishing vessel was on fire. The skipper of *Investor M* gave his position as ten nautical miles east-southeast of Blackhead, Northern Ireland. This position was disputed by Shane McNamara, the then lighthouse attendant on Mew Island which is approximately on these co-ordinates. *Watchdog 72*, a fisheries aircraft, identified the exact location and Donaghadee lifeboat altered course to the new co-ordinates. Some vessels were heading to the casualty, including Seacat Scotland and HSS Stena Voyager. At this time the skipper of *Investor* reported the fire was out but access to the engine room was impossible because of heat and smoke. He requested that he would need a tow to Bangor. The lifeboat took *Investor* in tow and arrived safely in Bangor.

May 16. A speedboat was broken down off Sandycove Caravan Park, Ballywalter. There were three persons on board with no flares, oars or paddles but all were wearing lifejackets. When the lifeboat arrived they had to launch the XP boat as the casualty was very close to the rocks and in imminent danger of being smashed to pieces. All three were taken on board and the lifeboat towed their boat to Donaghadee.

On approaching the harbour there was another call for assistance from yacht *Dyffedh of Myla*. The lifeboat escorted the yacht safely into harbour.

June 8. A call from the Belfast-Liverpool ferry *Lagan Viking* stating that a man had possibly gone overboard as he could not be found onboard. The lifeboat was launched in excellent visibility and flat calm conditions; an object in the water should have been easily spotted. As nothing was found and the time elapsed that anyone could have survived in the cold water, the Coastguard terminated the search.

June 14. Belfast Coastguard reported a small yacht with four persons on board on the rocks at Mew Island. The lifeboat used the XP class boat to ferry three survivors to the lifeboat and the fourth to the island where the former lifeboat mechanic Walker Simpson, now the lighthouse keeper, was able to provide accommodation for the rest of the day to await the next incoming tide. The lifeboat landed the survivors in Donaghadee. When the tide returned, the yacht refloated without damage.

June 22. A RIB had strayed on to the rocks north of Ballywalter en route home from Portpatrick. The lifeboat arrived on scene; the occupants were still on board although one had been in the water and was very cold, so the casualties were brought into the lifeboat. When the RIB was recovered it was brought to Donaghadee.

June 29. Call from a small sailing boat whose engine had broken down and, as there was no wind, the Coastguard decided to send the lifeboat in case the vessel drifted on to the Copelands. When *Saxon* got alongside they took a mother and child on board but the man did not take a tow as he said he was quite happy to carry on alone. The Coastguard monitored his progress and some time later he arrived in Donaghadee under his own sail.

July 28. A motor cruiser *Roxy Too* was en route from England to the Irish coast when their engines started to overheat. Several attempts were made to start the engines but this proved fruitless. The Coastguard was contacted, Donaghadee lifeboat was alerted, and proceeded to their position. The casualty was taken in tow and brought in without incident.

August 1. Information was received that *MV Islander* was taking water in Belfast Lough. Bangor inshore lifeboat was already on scene but Donaghadee lifeboat was asked to assist. On arrival Donaghadee lifeboat put a tow rope aboard and towed the vessel to Bangor Marina where it was lifted out of the water immediately.

August 8. A 999 call to Belfast Coastguard reported a jet ski drifting off Ballyferris Point. Donaghadee lifeboat *Saxon* was launched and proceeded to the area. The lifeboat conducted a search using flares and night vision equipment. Coastguards and police searched the shoreline for abandoned trailers or vehicles while a Puma helicopter assisted the lifeboat offshore. Nothing was found and the search was called off after several hours.

August 9. Coastguards received a 999 call that a canoeist was in difficulties off Ballyvester beach. When the lifeboat arrived on scene they had difficulty locating the casualty as the canoe was so low in the water and the boy was lying across it. When the lifeboat came alongside the casualty he was unable to move or help himself as he was suffering from severe hypothermia and close to unconsciousness. One of the lifeboat crew, Richard McGimpsey, entered the water and assisted him into the lifting sling. The boy was taken below deck and wrapped in blankets before the canoe was recovered. Ruth McNamara was contacted to meet the lifeboat to check the casualty over before the ambulance arrived. He was kept in hospital for observation. This definitely was a life saved; the casualty would not have lasted much longer in the water.

August 11. A mayday call to Belfast Coastguard stated that a 35 foot motor launch, *Princess Jenny*, was on the Briggs Reef at Groomsport, although this was later changed to Ballymacormick Point. There were five persons on board. Bangor lifeboat had been called out first and approached the casualty to take the occupants off and transfer them to the Donaghadee boat. Once this was done two crewmen, Shane McNamara and John Ashwood, went aboard the casualty to set up the tow to try and free her. *Saxon* brought her off the rocks easily and it was decided to take her to Bangor Marina. Shortly after the tow started Shane reported that they were taking water quite quickly; it was several inches above the carpets in the cabin and rising. As it was now after midnight it was not known if the crane man would be in the marina to hoist the casualty out, but luckily the vessel was lifted out immediately. The lifeboats returned to their bases at 1.15 am.

October 5. A 999 call reported a sailing boat capsized with three men in the water. The lifeboat was on scene in a few minutes and took the men aboard then, after some difficulty as the vessel was completely upside down, they managed to right it and assist the survivors to shore.

November 5. An urgent request from a large bulk carrier anchored in Bangor Bay to medivac a crew member who had taken ill. The casualty was already strapped in to the vessel's own stretcher and was transferred to the lifeboat and taken to Bangor Harbour to the waiting ambulance.

December 8. A mayday call from trawler *Aspire* stating they had been in collision with a smaller boat *Friscius.* The lifeboat launched immediately and proceeded to the area. Meanwhile *Aspire* had taken on board two survivors. *Friscius* had been holed and now rolled over and sank. *Aspire* left the area to land the survivors in Portavogie to a waiting ambulance. The lifeboat was asked to carry on to the scene to search for wreckage or anything likely to cause a danger to other vessels. Just a few fish boxes were found afloat but nothing else was discovered. Returned to base.

2004

January 11. Belfast Coastguard requested an immediate launch to assist Newcastle and Portaferry lifeboats in a search for a man who had fallen into the water off Killough harbour. While on passage to the scene they learned that Newcastle lifeboat had lost all engine power and had to anchor one mile offshore in Newcastle Bay. The Coastguard redirected the Donaghadee boat to attend to Newcastle lifeboat. They reached the scene at 5.45 pm and took the disabled lifeboat under tow to Ardglass harbour, before returning to the search area. At 9.30 pm the search was stood down until the next morning but sadly nothing was found. The body was washed ashore some days later.

February 21. The Coastguard received a 999 call saying that a car had driven into the harbour. The pagers were used to assemble the crew. The driver had thrown his driver's licence to a lady walking on the pier before accelerating off the edge into the water just beside the lifeboat moorings. Three of the crew jumped into the boarding boat, recovered the man and immediately tried to resuscitate him. Ruth arrived and worked with the casualty until the ambulance men took over but to no avail. A police diving team checked the vehicle to confirm no other person was inside.

March 24. A jet ski was seen from the boathouse to be in difficulty and a immediate launch was ordered. This service went without a hitch; one female was brought aboard the lifeboat, the jet ski towed to harbour and the lifeboat was back on the mooring in twenty one minutes.

June 16. Coastguards reported a small rowing boat in a sinking condition offshore at Ballywhiskin, Millisle with one occupant aboard. On nearing the scene the lifeboat crew could see the casualty had gone down and the young man had managed to scramble onto some outlying rocks which would soon be covered by the incoming tide. The lifeboat's XP boat was made ready and launched to recover the man from the rocks. The teenager was very cold, confused and shocked. On arrival at Donaghadee he was examined by Dr Neill and the ambulance paramedics before going home with his father.

June 19. Coastguard responded to a mayday call from a small fishing boat *Sea Gypsy* with five men on board reporting a loss of power and taking water. The lifeboat launched and was on scene in twenty minutes, immediately taking four of the casualties who were suffering badly from seasickness onboard the lifeboat. Two lifeboatmen with the salvage pump were transferred to *Sea Gypsy*, and tow was then started towards Carrickfergus, completed without further incident.

July 15. The Coastguard contacted the lifeboat secretary with details of a sixteen metre motor cruiser *Elgin Dragon* which had lost all power twenty five miles south east of the station. The estimated time to the casualty was one hour and, when on scene, the lifeboat took the cruiser in tow and set course for Peel Harbour, Isle of Man. On nearing the harbour they were met by the Peel lifeboat which assisted in securing the casualty alongside. After refuelling at Peel, Donaghadee lifeboat returned to station.

August 15. A small sailing boat had grounded on outlying rocks four miles south of Donaghadee. The weather was calm with very slight sea conditions. It was impossible for the two crew to get to shore and they would probably lose their boat, so the lifeboat was launched and was on scene in a few minutes. They sent the XP boat in with a line and gently hauled the sailing boat off the rocks with only minimal damage. The casualty was then able to sail to Donaghadee escorted by the lifeboat.

August 21. A yacht, *Robins Dream,* reported being disabled by old fishing nets entangled in its propeller. The lifeboat towed the casualty to Donaghadee with the crew still aboard. The yachtsmen, with the use of borrowed diving gear, cut the nets away and released the prop; no serious damage was done.

August 29. While returning from a PR exercise at Portavogie, the lifeboat was contacted by the Coastguard. The motor boat *Annalla* had its propeller snagged on a rope and was unable to release it. The lifeboat arrived on scene about twenty five minutes later and proceeded to tow the casualty to Carrickfergus without incident.

October 13. A 999 call reported a red-hulled yacht, *Rambling Rose,* aground on the Briggs Reef near Groomsport. Before the lifeboat reached the casualty the yacht's crew managed to dislodge it from the reef assisted by the rising tide, then set course for Bangor Marina escorted by the lifeboat.

October 24. *Saxon* was on a training exercise four miles north-west of

Saxon in Donaghadee Harbour

Donaghadee when Coastguards asked for assistance. A RIB, *Sea Mist,* had apparently broken a drive shaft and was drifting close to Portavogie. The lifeboat came alongside about twenty five minutes later, took the occupant aboard the lifeboat and towed the RIB to Donaghadee.

November 11. Fishing boat *Emerald Dawn* reported to be sinking. The lifeboat crew was assembled in the boathouse at 3 am to be briefed by the Coastguard regarding search patterns. The scene was over forty miles south of the station and would take almost two hours to reach. Newcastle and Clogherhead lifeboats were also in the search along with fourteen fishing vessels from Kilkeel and Annalong. Donaghadee lifeboat was the on scene commander. Some time later a liferaft was spotted by a merchant ship and a survivor was air lifted by helicopter to hospital in Douglas, Isle of Man. Donaghadee lifeboat was relieved at 6 pm. Refuelled at Kilkeel and returned to station.

December 6. Belfast Coastguard asked if Donaghadee lifeboat would be prepared to assist with a compassionate callout. The fourteen year old child of a crewman on board the fishing vessel *Boy Stewart* had been killed in a road traffic accident. The lifeboat was asked to intercept the vessel and bring the man ashore to Portavogie. It was decided to contact Dr Neill in case the man suffered shock. The lifeboat rendezvoused with the trawler and took aboard Mr John Nixon and set course for Portavogie, where the Coastguard had arranged a police car to take him to the hospital where his son was.

Saxon in action

2005   April 22. A distress message was heard by the Coastguard from the yacht *RagTag* informing them that a rope had gone overboard and fouled the propeller and that they were drifting towards the rocks at Burial Island near Ballyhalbert. Radio contact was very poor between the yacht and the lifeboat, and the heavy swells in the area coupled with the darkness made the casualty hard to locate. The Coastguard was able to relay a new position, approximately one mile north of Burial Island. The towrope was passed and tow commenced for Donaghadee where the doctor examined the yachtsmen for shock and hypothermia.

May 1. Fishing vessel *Athena* reported engine failure two miles east of Portavogie. *Saxon* launched and proceeded to the position. After the tow was connected the coxswain decided that in the heavy conditions the narrow entrance at Portavogie Harbour would be too dangerous so course was set for Donaghadee.

June 8. A member of the public reported two children stranded on the rocks off Millisle beach. The person reporting the incident stayed on the line and, as it was getting dark, was able to direct the lifeboat to the scene. The XP boat was launched and one child at a time was put aboard the lifeboat where they enjoyed the trip to Donaghadee.

June 12. The lifeboat was called to assist a RIB which had lost power approximately fifteen miles east of Ballywalter. The casualty was located and towed back to its home base of Portavogie.

June 17. This callout was for another RIB used for angling, which was drifting approximately two miles east of Mew Island lighthouse. The casualty had lost engine power, and the lifeboat was on the scene in under twelve minutes, proceeding to tow the RIB to Bangor Marina.

June 19. The lifeboat was asked to assist in a search for a small speedboat which was three hours overdue at Portpatrick. There had been no contact from the casualty and all the Search and Rescue organisations were tasked. Donaghadee lifeboat was to proceed towards the Scottish coast and a helicopter and an RAF Nimrod was also alerted. Shortly after the Donaghadee boat launched, the Portpatrick boat found the casualty with all the occupants fit and well.

June 30. An EPIRB (a radio beacon which operates automatically if immersed in water and gives the name of the vessel and its position) broadcast was picked up by Belfast Coastguard who requested an immediate launch. The EPIRB was from a fishing trawler *Auriga* which had been fishing approximately ten miles off Portavogie. Coastguards asked for the assistance of all vessels in the area, and a helicopter was dispatched to the area. A ferry, *North Sea Trader,* spotted what they thought was a large buoy or a liferaft and, on getting closer, they confirmed it was a raft with two men aboard. Shortly afterwards Donaghadee lifeboat came alongside and transferred the survivors to the lifeboat. One of the men's fathers had previously been lost at sea. The lifeboat returned the men to their home port of Portavogie.

July 1. The next day the Coastguard again asked the lifeboat to assist with the *Auriga's* EPIRB as it was still transmitting and needed to be retrieved and disabled. The lifeboat found the beacon and retuned to station.

July 24. Just three days before this incident the lifeboat crew and the ambulance team had carried out an extended exercise with new equipment including a 'vacuum' stretcher for use in transporting patients over rough ground.

The Coastguard advised the station that two people had been injured in a fall on Copeland Island and needed medical attention. Luckily both Dr Robert Neill and Ruth McNamara were available to attend the casualties. On arrival at the island the full details became clear. The man had fallen from a flag mast where he had been replacing flag halliards. On hearing him fall his wife ran from the house and tripped, splitting her head on a rock. After treatment by the doctor and paramedic, each casualty was carried down by stretcher over very rough terrain to the shore and then onto the lifeboat. On arrival in harbour the casualties were transferred to ambulances and taken to hospital. One was released the next day, the other several days later.

July 25. Launched to a small Shetland cabin cruiser with engine failure, and towed to Donaghadee.

September 9. The lifeboat was called to assist two men whose boat had grounded on Copeland Island the previous evening due to power failure. The men had slept rough under some sheets of wood but as the weather turned foul they started to get very cold and called for help. The lifeboat picked up the men and their boat and landed them safely in Donaghadee.

November 7. Donaghadee and Bangor lifeboats were alerted to a fishing vessel that was taking water one mile off Bangor pier. The inshore lifeboat stood by as the casualty limped slowly into Bangor harbour. When the vessel was made fast, Donaghadee crewmen boarded with the salvage pump and cleared the engine room.

2006

January 12. At 8 pm a message was received from a fishing vessel *Giolla na Mara* saying they had an engine failure off Portavogie. The lifeboat launched immediately, proceeding south toward the casualty. In the meantime a local boat came alongside and offered assistance. The trouble was traced to a blocked fuel line which was cleared and the engine restarted just as the lifeboat arrived. As the wind was gusting to gale force and the sea very rough, the coxswain asked if they wanted to be escorted into Portavogie. The skipper declined the offer and said they would carry on to their home port of Killybegs. The lifeboat provided an escort as far as Mew Island before returning to station. Regular contact was maintained between the trawler and the Coastguard as it travelled north. There was no further incident.

March 12. At 1 am the Coastguard advised the station that a Russian merchant ship *Sesam* was adrift in the middle of the North Channel with a loss of power. Her angle of drift was north-northwesterly and it was decided the lifeboat would not be needed until 5 am when the ship would be nearing Mew Island. Both Larne and Donaghadee lifeboats were asked to stand by and launched at 4 am. At this time it was estimated that the drift would take her clear of Mew Island by three miles.

Donaghadee lifeboat had to return to harbour to land a crewman who had sustained a head injury in the extremely rough conditions. After landing the crewman into the care of Dr Neill and making up crew numbers they returned to stand by the casualty. Arrangements had been made with the Irish Lights Tender *Granuaille* to tow *Sesam* to a place of refuge. Larne lifeboat passed the tow rope to the casualty and was then released and returned to base. Progress was very slow at first because of the poor conditions but eventually the ship was anchored in Bangor Bay and Donaghadee lifeboat returned to station.

June 1. A call to launch from Belfast Coastguard to assist a twin masted yacht *Ti Gitu* off Donaghadee Harbour. They had something tangled in their propeller and were only making very slow headway. The lifeboat escorted the casualty into harbour without incident.

June 20. Just before midday the station mechanic Shane McNamara and harbour workman Ian McDowell spotted a man in his mid-60s acting strangely, eventually putting to sea in an inflatable similar to those sold for children in supermarkets. It was obvious the man was drunk and was now setting off with more drink. Despite the recklessness of his actions the would be sailor was at least wearing a lifejacket. He didn't seem to have any means of communications and probably hadn't told anyone of his intentions. Shane alerted his brother, coxswain Philip Mc-Namara who in turn alerted the launching authority. It was decided to launch immediately and in the space of ten-fifteen minutes the dinghy had drifted over a mile. The man insisted he was in no danger but the coxswain disagreed and he was brought aboard the lifeboat along with his dinghy and returned to shore.

July 7. A 999 call reported three persons in the water off Millisle beach after a canoe capsized. It appeared that two children had overturned the canoe, neither of whom were wearing lifejackets. A thirty three year old man had swum out to attempt to rescue them and one of the children swam ashore unaided but the other child could not swim and the young man assisted in keeping the boy afloat. The lifeboat was on scene twenty seven minutes after the 999 call was received. After using the small XP boat to haul the man and child out of the water they returned to Don-aghadee harbour to hand over to the ambulance service. The child was suffering from hypothermia and was very shocked.

July 11. A local man who was obviously very drunk made his way down the harbour and eventually climbed down the ladder into his own boat, where he fiddled about for some time, before falling overboard into the sea. This had been observed by several people including the lifeboat cox-swain Philip McNamara who was in his own boat with his son Able and immediately went to help. At first the man refused any help but eventually Philip and Able got a hold on him and pulled him aboard then took him to the steps where he was helped ashore.

August 16. A 999 call reported a man stranded on offshore rocks at Millisle by the incoming tide. *Saxon* was launched and the XP boat was used to recover the casualty who was well and unhurt. The lifeboat landed the man in Donaghadee without further incident.

August 22. A 999 call alerted Belfast Coastguard of a man in the water at Orlock Head, Portavo. The Coastguard immediately launched both Bangor and Donaghadee lifeboats. Both lifeboats reached the scene together, and Bangor inshore lifeboat pulled the apparently lifeless casualty on board and immediately transferred him to the larger boat where the crew was waiting with first aid equipment. One of the Bangor crew also came aboard to help with the casualty. The coxswain then instructed the ambulance to meet them in Donaghadee harbour. While on passage the mechanic detected a faint pulse; the crew placed him in the recovery position when he began to vomit lots of sea water. He had a badly bleeding head wound which the crew attended to. The paramedics came aboard and started to prepare the casualty to be brought ashore. They placed him in a vacuum stretcher, a piece of equipment which impressed the lifeboat crew greatly; this incident showed the value of having one aboard the lifeboat. The casualty was in poor condition and, despite the earlier signs, seemed to deteriorate before he was taken to the ambulance; in hospital his condition was described as critical but late in the afternoon on August 23 he regained consciousness. Belfast Coastguard thanked both crews for the excellent work they had done.

August 24. Reports of a RIB with engine failure and requiring assistance halfway between Donaghadee and Portpatrick. *Saxon* was launched and was alongside the casualty in twenty five minutes and, as the RIB's engine still would not start, the lifeboat towed it back to harbour without incident.

September 1. Coastguard reported a small boat adrift with three boys on board offshore at Ballywalter. Lifeboat located the casualty and towed it to Ballywalter harbour.

November 1. The lifeboat was launched to go to the aid of a possible suicide attempt at Ballyhalbert harbour, but was eventually recalled as the body was retrieved by Coastguards and police.

November 18. A report from a fishing vessel with engine failure one mile offshore at Ballywalter and needing assistance. Lifeboat launched

Saxon powers out of Donaghadee Harbour

and was alongside in approximately twenty minutes. The vessel was towed into harbour without incident.

February 7. Belfast Coastguard requested a launch to a fishing trawler which had lost engine power in mid channel. The weather at the time was squally with poor visibility. The wind was south-east gale force, with very rough seas. The lifeboat proceeded to the casualty at reduced speed due to the severe conditions. When they arrived on scene it was hard to communicate with the casualty as the deck crew of four were non-English speaking and only the skipper could speak English. Eventually a tow rope was attached and the lifeboat proceeded slowly to Bangor harbour.

2007

April 1. A report of a canoeist being overdue. After a search the casualty was found. It turned out the man was an experienced canoeist but had been caught in a strong tide and was unable to make headway despite his best efforts. The lifeboat took the man and his canoe on board and landed them safely in Donaghadee.

May 23. The Coastguard informed the launching officer that there was a man in the water at Ballywhiskin, four miles away. The lifeboat arrived on scene quickly and recovered the man from the water, returning him safely to Donaghadee.

June 3. A phone call from the skipper of motor launch *Mermaid* direct to the station saying that his engine had broken down just offshore at Mew Island. He had seven persons plus himself on board. On arrival the passengers were transferred to the lifeboat, the skipper staying on board *Mermaid* during the tow to Donaghadee.

June 28. A small leisure craft called to say they had lost power and were drifting. The sea was choppy with a force 4-5 westerly wind. They had a spare engine aboard but could not get it mounted because of the severe motion of the boat. Donaghadee lifeboat was launched and located them quickly. Towed them into Groomsport which was the nearest harbour.

July 22. A jet ski had broken down off Millisle beach. On arrival the lifeboat discovered three persons in the water. They were taken aboard the lifeboat and were landed along with their jet ski in Donaghadee.

July 26. A man, out on an angling trip, called the Coastguard by mobile phone saying he needed assistance. The lifeboat was alongside the casualty in less than thirty minutes and first aid was given. The man had hurt his back and was quite cold, showing signs of mild hypothermia. The man and his boat were taken ashore where he was transferred to an ambulance.

July 29. A vessel en route from Portpatrick to Bangor became detached from the rest of the boats during the annual RIB raid and was unsure of its position. The crew contacted Belfast Coastguard by mobile and Donaghadee lifeboat was launched. The wind was force five north-west with a heavy swell, which made it very difficult for the lifeboat to spot them. The occupants were asked to fire a flare which was then seen by the lifeboat. The RIB was not taken in tow but was safely escorted to Donaghadee.

August 12. Call from the Coastguard reporting a missing person, believed to be in the water at Millisle three miles south of Donaghadee. The lifeboat fired four parachute flares to illuminate the area but nothing was found. Just as the crew launched the XP boat to search inshore in the shallow water, the Coastguard notified the lifeboat that the person had been brought ashore safely. The lifeboat returned to base.

August 28. The Coastguard asked for assistance for a leisure boat which had broken down near the Briggs Reef at Groomsport. On the way to the scene the lifeboat spotted the casualty in a different position, nearer to Donaghadee. A tow was connected and proceeded to harbour.

September 2. Report of a small boat adrift in a dangerous position off the Copeland Island with apparent engine failure. The lifeboat arrived on scene very quickly and could see that in a very short time the casualty was being swept into a strong tide race. In the coxswain's opinion they had taken no precautions and were ill-prepared for their trip. On return to harbour the Coastguard spoke to the occupants and advised them to take better precautions and more suitable equipment. The boat had not been used for years and the engine had not been serviced. There is no doubt that without the lifeboat's help this boat would have been swamped close to their location.

September 7. Coastguard was informed directly by mobile phone that a small boat had an engine failure off Ballywalter and needed help. The lifeboat towed the vessel to near the harbour entrance, where the XP boat completed the tow into the harbour as the tide was very low which prevented the lifeboat from entering.

October 12. Lifeboat was launched to the aid of a 36 foot motor boat at 11.30 pm. The vessel *Spice Trader* had suffered engine failure. When the lifeboat arrived on scene a tow rope and crewman, George Thompson, were put on board to assist with the tow which proceeded to Donaghadee without incident.

December 22. The next call for the lifeboat was quite tricky as the casualty had found itself in shallow water between some rocks. The lifeboat managed to get a heaving line to the casualty and pulled them out backwards to deeper water and then on to Donaghadee.

2008

March 17. The lifeboat was called to tug *Kingston* which had machinery problems and was at risk of fire. The tug was at the entrance to Belfast Channel. On the way to the casualty the lifeboat's fire pumps were made ready. Once it was established there was no risk of fire, the tug's skipper requested the lifeboat to manoeuvre the tug alongside the large barge they had been towing. This was done using the lifeboat's two engines and the tug's bow thruster in readiness for the tow back to Belfast by one of the harbour tugs. At this point the lifeboat left the scene.

May 8. The Coastguard informed the lifeboat that a speedboat with three people on board was broken down near Orlock Head. The lifeboat was on scene in fifteen minutes and the casualty was towed to Donaghadee without incident.

May 25. Three canoeists had left Donaghadee to paddle to the Copeland Island. It was a fine clear morning, but a short time into their trip they found themselves in a strong tidal race with steep waves and were in real

Saxon takes part in a training exercise

danger of swamping or capsizing. At this time they were seen by the lifeboat which was on a training exercise. Two canoes and their occupants were taken aboard the lifeboat and the other was escorted to shore. The lifeboat resumed its training exercise.

May 31. A 6.5 m power boat with three persons and a dog on board asked for the assistance of the lifeboat as they had engine failure. Their location was only a mile from Donaghadee, and the casualty was recovered quickly and brought to harbour.

July 2. A message was received from the Belfast-Birkenhead ferry *Lagan Viking* that a possible medivac was required, so the lifeboat launched with Dr Neill aboard. The ferry turned to provide a lee for the lifeboat to come alongside safely with both vessels proceeding at five knots. The doctor boarded the *Lagan Viking* and reported back that he had examined the patient and found him suffering from a skin infection. The doctor advised the man to stay on board and continue his journey to Birkenhead. Because of the patient's previous medical history, it would have been too dangerous to try to transfer him down the ship's side by ladder.

July 4. Coastguard requested an immediate launch to assist a small yacht, a GP14 which had capsized and two persons, both adults, a male and female, were in the water. The lifeboat was on scene in fifteen minutes, by which time a jet ski rider had recovered the female to the back of the jet ski, and the male was clinging to a rope attached to the jet ski. Two crewmen, Richard McGimpsey and George Thompson, entered the water to recover the casualties to the lifeboat. The man was suffering from severe hypothermia and showing signs of confusion and incoherence. The girl was then brought aboard the lifeboat for return to Donaghadee where two waiting ambulances transferred them to hospital.

July 17. This rescue took place during the Civil Service dispute, so there is no exact position. The casualty was approximately one mile off-shore, probably fishing. He called the Coastguard reporting engine failure and the lifeboat was launched immediately. The casualty was taken under tow and returned to Donaghadee.

August 4. A 999 call to the Coastguard from the casualty which was approximately one mile north of Burr Point. It had apparent engine failure, possibly out of fuel. The lifeboat was launched and proceeded to the casualty on a flat calm sea, arriving on scene at 17.53 where the fishing protection vessel *Ken Vickers* had already put a line onto the casualty. Donaghadee lifeboat took over the tow and set course for home. Arrived back in harbour and was immediately ready for service.

August 17. The Coastguard paged the lifeboat crew to a child in distress. She was in a small rubber dinghy and had been blown offshore. The lifeboat crew decided to launch the boarding boat, as the casualty was close inshore and only a few hundred metres from the base. The boarding boat was dispatched and arrived on scene at the same time as a canoe, who attached a line and towed the casualty to shore. The boarding boat returned to base.

August 23. The Coastguard requested the assistance of Donaghadee lifeboat to a yacht which had lost engine power and the persons on board were feeling the effects of the worsening weather conditions. The lifeboat was launched and headed for the supposed location of the yacht, eleven nautical miles north east of Donaghadee. As it happened, the casualty was quite some distance from there and was eventually located approximately sixteen nautical miles north-northeast, with the nearest point to return the casualty being Larne. Larne all-weather lifeboat met Donaghadee lifeboat at Browns Bay and rendered assistance. Larne inshore lifeboat also rendered assistance at the mooring. After a short break in Larne, Donaghadee set course for home but was diverted to another incident.

Assistance was requested from the Coastguard for an eleven metre yacht in distress and the coordinates of the casualty were close to the passage route for Donaghadee lifeboat. The yacht was taken under tow to Bangor Harbour and the lifeboat returned to base without further incident where she was refuelled and ready for service shortly after midnight.

September 1. Call from the Coastguard reporting casualty in distress approximately four nautical miles east of Donaghadee. The casualty type was given as a yacht but was in fact a cabin cruiser. The casualty was undertaking a delivery passage when she encountered gearbox difficulties and lost propulsion. The lifeboat was directed to correct the coordinates and took the casualty under tow and brought her and two crew safely ashore to Donaghadee without further incident.

September 3. A 999 call to the Coastguard reported two small punts missing offshore off Ballywalter harbour with four persons on board. The lifeboat was launched immediately and the deputy launching authority was informed. The lifeboat reached the casualty search area and had to use search lights and night vision glasses to locate the vessels. Four young males were onboard with no means of communication other than one mobile phone. They had no lifejackets or distress flares. The mobile phone was used to speak with the lifeboat as the casualties could see the lifeboat, which could not initially see the casualty. They had one small engine that did not work along with one oar between them. The persons, along with their vessels, were brought aboard the lifeboat and returned immediately to shore at Donaghadee.

September 7. A 999 call to the Coastguard informing of an elderly man in the water off Donaghadee shore front. The Coastguard was already in communication with Bangor lifeboat which was diverted to the scene but assistance from Donaghadee lifeboat was requested immediately.

As the casualty was in shallow water, the lifeboat boarding boat was launched with a crew of five. As the lifeboat boarding boat approached the scene, the man left the water of his own accord and the boat returned to the station. It later transpired that this same man had already been rescued by the police and ambulance earlier in the morning but the incident had not been reported to the Coastguard.

2009

March 22. *Saxon* was launched and the coxswain spoke with Bangor inshore lifeboat which was already afloat and had also been tasked to this incident. Donaghadee lifeboat proceeded at full speed and the Donaghadee coxswain instructed Bangor ILB to continue ahead at full speed to assist the casualty, which was stranded on rocks with three persons on board. Bangor ILB lifted the three persons off the rocks as Donaghadee lifeboat, five minutes behind Bangor ILB, continued south towards the casualty. Bangor ILB towed the vessel off the rocks and into Ballywalter Harbour. *Saxon* stood by until the service was completed by Bangor ILB, and, as there was no further incident, Donaghadee lifeboat returned to station.

May 23. Coastguard asked Donaghadee lifeboat for assistance to a casualty stranded on rocks just 250m from the station. Due to the close proximity, it was prudent to use the lifeboat boarding vessel, with George Thomson and Tony Simmonds on board, to access the casualty. On arrival at the scene, the lifeboat put a line to the casualty vessel and eased it off the rocks. Only slight damage was caused to the rudder of the casualty vessel during its time on the rocks, and no further damage seemed to have been caused by either lifeboat or tender. Once safely off the rocks, the casualty continued into the marina under its own power as the lifeboat stood by. The lifeboat returned to base without further incident.

June 13. A Shetland day boat had set out for Millisle, just four miles from Donaghadee, on a sea angling trip with for male adults on board. They were ill prepared in that they had not checked the engine or fuel supply, they had no charts or flares, they were wearing buoyancy aids but not proper life jackets and only one of their mobile phones were working. They planned to go deep sea fishing where mobile phones may not have worked, and they had no VHF radio. Furthermore, there were only two seats on board for the four adults.

The casualty called the coastguard using a 999 call and reported that they had broken down. They were not sure of their position, but guessed they were heading into Belfast Lough, round the back of the Copeland Islands. *Saxon* was launched and proceeded to the general area. The sea was flat calm and visibility was excellent, so the casualty was quickly and easily seen; just off Groomsport at the entrance to Belfast Lough. The lifeboat took the survivors aboard and attached a towline to the casualty vessel and towed it back to Donaghadee. There was no further incident and the survivors were interviewed by the coastguard.

June 14. 12.20 hours. Immediate launch requested from the coastguard as a flare had been reported less than a mile off Millisle. The lifeboat arrived at the casualty in just a few minutes. It appeared that the crew of the vessel had accidentally dropped their hand-held VHF radio overboard and, in a moment of haste, fired a flare. There had been no real danger and the casualty was not in any real difficulty. The crew of the casualty vessel apologised for the inconvenience and the lifeboat returned to base.

Returning from service on 8th August 2009, the crew on *Saxon* (l-r): Deputy Launching Officer Murdoch Bennett, Mechanic Shane McNamara, Michael Field, Ross Bennett, John Allen, John Ashwood (seated), George Hackworth, John Petrie, Richard McGimpsey. On steps: Alfie McCulla, Coxswain Philip McNamara

June 14. 17.33 hours. This was exactly the same casualty as the previous day. It was even almost exactly the same location, although this time there were just three persons on board. All were returned to Donaghadee, along with the casualty vessel. The survivors were interviewed again by the coastguard, who said they were very unhappy with the lack of preparation and reliability of the craft. The crew were told not to put to sea again without better preparation. There was no further incident.

June 19. The Coastguard requested the launch of Donaghadee lifeboat to a yacht off Ballyhalbert. The casualty was close inshore, with the wind too light to sail safely, and with a failed engine. The lifeboat attached a towrope to the casualty vessel with the survivors remaining on board. Although Portavogie was the closest safe harbour, it made sense to bring the casualty to Donaghadee as that was the direction they were headed, the lifeboat did not need to divert and could return direct to base. The casualty was easy to tow and there were no further incidents.

June 27. The Coastguard requested the launch of *Saxon* to the casualty vessel, which had broken down just off the Copeland Islands. There were six people on board and the engine could not be restarted. The lifeboat proceeded immediately and arrived on the scene within a few minutes. A towline was attached and the casualty was towed to Groomsport with the survivors still on board the casualty vessel. On arrival back at Groomsport, the casualty was able to restart the engines and was able to berth under her own power. *Saxon* returned to base with no further incident.

Author's note

While this chapter must draw to a close, the good work of Donaghadee lifeboat continues, and will continue to do so for many years to come. The RNLI is an organisation like no other, with men and women voluntarily giving of their time to help others in times of need, and I would like to take this opportunity to comment on the courage, commitment, professionalism and bravery shown by the crew members with whom I had the privilege to go to sea. I also would like to mention that some crew members who served with me have progressed to become coxswains and mechanics within the RNLI. Hopefully I played a small part in helping and inspiring them along their pathways to success.

My time serving with the RNLI were happy years. I would like to mention my wife Margaret who had to put up with me all those years dashing off in the middle of the night, running out of family weddings to go on the lifeboat (not our own thankfully!) and refusing to go on many family holidays because of my commitment to the RNLI. No-one else would have tolerated it. She probably did as she had been used to it while growing up; her father was also coxswain. My greatest disappointment was having to retire as coxswain at 55 years old.

I am very proud to have been involved with the work of the RNLI for 37 years and often reflect on the people I have met and the life-long friends I have made from many stations throughout Ireland and beyond. I developed close ties with Bangor, Portrush, Howth and Ballyglass Lifeboat stations (to name but a few). Many Divisional Inspectors became friends and I hold them in the highest esteem. I have watched with interest the development of the lifeboats and the vast improvements in crew training over the years.

As recorded in this book I had to avail of the services of Donaghadee lifeboat on more than one occasion myself and I may not be here today if it were not for their swift and appropriate care in dealing with me when I suffered a cardiac condition whilst at the Mew Island.

I would like to dedicate this book to all the past, present and future lifeboat men and women in Donaghadee Lifeboat station. Their dedication to saving lives at sea is an inspiration to all.

Dear Reader

I hope you have enjoyed this publication from Ballyhay Books, an imprint of Laurel Cottage Ltd. We publish an eclectic mix of books, ranging from personal memoirs to authoritative books on local history, from sport to poultry, from photographs to fiction and from music to marine interests – but all with a distinctly local flavour.

To see details of these books as well as the beautifully illustrated books of our sister imprint, Cottage Publications, why not visit our website at

www.cottage-publications.com

or contact us at:–

Laurel Cottage
15 Ballyhay Rd
Donaghadee
Co. Down
N. Ireland
BT21 0NG
Tel: +44 (0)28 9188 8033

Timothy & Johnston

BALLYHAY BOOKS